May Go
M

THE GREA

THE GREAT TRANSFORMATION

The Sanctification and Glorification of the Believer

Maurice Roberts

And be not conformed to this world: but be ye transformed by the renewing of your mind, that ye may prove what is that good, and acceptable, and perfect, will of God.— Romans 12:2.

THE BANNER OF TRUTH TRUST

THE BANNER OF TRUTH TRUST

Head Office
3 Murrayfield Road
Edinburgh
EH12 6EL
UK

North America Office
PO Box 621
Carlisle
PA 17013
USA

banneroftruth.org

The eight sermons in this book were first published in
Sanctification and Glorification
(Reformation Book Centre, Adelaide, 1997)

*

ISBN
Print: 978 1 84871 914 9
EPUB: 978 1 84871 916 3
Kindle: 978 1 84871 917 0

*

Typeset in 11/15 Adobe Garamond Pro
at The Banner of Truth Trust, Edinburgh

Printed in the USA by
Versa Press Inc.,
East Peoria, IL.

Contents

Preface

The sermons which make up this little book were preached abroad at a conference over twenty years ago. I would like to make them available now to a wider readership because I am convinced that the doctrines of sanctification and glorification are, in a sad non-religious day like our own, a great encouragement to God's beloved people. God's children here go through a multitude of trials and discouragements. But 'our light affliction is but for a moment.' All true believers in Christ have left behind them the state of sin and death. What believers now have to look forward to is the blessed change from grace to glory. The author's wish and prayer is that readers will be refreshed, encouraged, and reinvigorated as they lift up their eyes to future comforts and joys in eternity.

MAURICE ROBERTS
Inverness, July 2019

ONE

Living When Sin Abounds

And because iniquity shall abound, the love of many shall wax cold. But he that shall endure unto the end, the same shall be saved.—Matt. 24:12, 13.

The general subject which binds these addresses together is that of sanctification and glorification, and I shall begin by saying a little about the importance of these two great themes.

They are, of course, quite distinct insofar as sanctification belongs to this present life, whereas glorification belongs to the world to come for the people of God. Sanctification is in time, but glorification will be in eternity. Sanctification is a long process. It begins at the new birth and it continues all the way through life until we come to death. Glorification, on the other hand, will be an instantaneous act of God by which the soul at death is made perfect. Then the body with the soul will be made fully perfect in the day of resurrection.

So sanctification is glorification begun, and glorification will be sanctification completed. Sanctification is glorification in the bud, but glorification will be sanctification in full flower.

The degree to which we are sanctified in this life will have a bearing upon the amount of glory conferred upon us in the world to come. There is no reason to doubt that. Just as in this life no two Christians are at the same stage of sanctification, so in glory no two saints will be identical in the measure of their glory. Some will have more, and some less.

In very sobering words, Robert Murray M'Cheyne said that every sin committed after conversion takes away something from our glorious reward in heaven. That is something which we in our modern world would do well to pause and consider, and it really brings us to the importance of this theme. If you and I long to be close to the throne of God in glory, we must study holiness and obedience to God now, in this life, because without holiness no man shall see the Lord.

We see that Christ speaks of both sanctification and glorification in our text in Matthew 24:13. 'He that shall endure unto the end' refers to the process of sanctification. He who continues steadfast in the faith unto the end of his life shall receive salvation. And the salvation looked at there is not salvation in the sense of the beginning of it, but in the sense of the completion and fulfilment of it. It refers to the reward of glory in heaven itself.

This text comes from a sermon of Christ's which we refer to as his great discourse on the end of the world. Not all commentators have understood this chapter in that sense. Some regard Christ's words as having reference not to the end of the world, but to the end of the Jewish state, which was destroyed by the Romans in AD 70. That is because of something Christ says in verse 34: 'Verily I say unto you, This generation shall not pass, till all these things be fulfilled.' Some people have looked at that word 'generation' and have concluded that Christ must have been speaking of people who were then living on earth, as though he were saying, 'All that I am saying to you will have its fulfilment in the lifetime of men and women living in the world today.'

How are we to answer that objection? In Scripture, the word 'generation' has more senses than one. One of the senses of the word is 'nation', and I believe that Bishop J. C. Ryle had the correct interpretation of it when he related it to the Jews as a *nation*. So Christ is not saying that all his words here will be completed by AD 70 when the Jewish state is destroyed, but rather he is talking about what will occur at the end of the world, because at the end of the world the Jewish people will still be a distinct nation.

Therefore, I believe that this sermon of Christ's is a prophecy of what will take place in the history of the world during this Christian age between the first coming and the second coming of Christ. I do not think we can seriously doubt that because at verse 30 Christ refers to the Son of Man appearing in heaven, coming in the clouds with power and great glory, and gathering out his elect (verse 31) from the nations. Obviously he is not speaking about the end of the Old Testament age; he is speaking about the end of the world and the end of time. That, then, is the background and the context in which the words of my text are found in verses 12 and 13: 'Because iniquity shall abound, the love of *many* shall wax [or 'grow'] cold. But he that shall endure unto the end, the same shall be saved.'

This is a text which is of great importance to us as believers in this life. It tells us in the first place that there are some ages in the history of the world when iniquity will abound. To 'abound' means to overflow. So there are some ages in the history of the world when evil will become extreme and when it will become intensely difficult for the people of God to maintain their standards of obedience to his word. There will be, says Christ, some ages in the history of the world when Satan will be especially let loose, when all the powers of hell will be in conflict with the cause of Christ on earth.

Now we know that that is not always so. There are some periods in the history of the world when sin does not abound in this sense. The world is always evil, and the devil always goes about to do mischief, but it is not true to say that in every age of mankind sin and wickedness are as great and as powerful as they sometimes are. There is a sort of ebb and flow in the powers of hell and of darkness. The forces of evil upon the people of God in this life fluctuate, and we are to expect that.

Let me bring this into our modern world. Here is how I understand what has been happening in Britain during the twentieth century. Before the First World War we began to lose our Christian doctrine and our Christian theology. If you go back to the nineteenth century, Christian ideas and ideals, Christian laws and standards, and Christian doctrines and practices were understood. They were known and prized. But about the time of the First World War these doctrines came under a tremendous attack from liberalism, modernism and the higher criticism. The powers of hell were doing their utmost to destroy Christian teaching in the state, in the schools and in society. Doctrine was being cast out.

But if you pass over the years and come to the period immediately after—at and after the Second World War—you see something else just as sinister: you see an attack being made upon Christian laws and the standards of morality which had previously been accepted by the country. So at the beginning of the twentieth century you could say that Christian doctrine came under attack, but by the 1960s it was the morality, the laws, the practices and the outworkings of Christianity that were being overturned. We are suffering today from the aftermath of that tremendous assault upon the gospel in the English-speaking world.

An illustration will make this matter still clearer. Imagine a river which in the summer time is a mere trickle of water in the river bed—just a tiny stream of water, not dangerous in any way or threatening. Nobody is afraid of that. There is no need for flood warnings to be issued by the government authorities. But you come back in the autumn or winter, or the spring when the snow is melting, and that trickle becomes a great flood and carries all before it. It breaks down trees, bridges and fences.

That is what our Lord is talking about: there are some periods in history when iniquity will abound and overflow. Sin will have a tremendous influence upon society. That will not always be the case. Sometimes sin will flow like a little rivulet or trickle; it will not be threatening. But in other generations sin will be a mighty force that will threaten to carry everything before it.

Confusion is widespread in society. People do not know where they are, what to believe, what is right or wrong, or what to understand concerning God. Religions and churches are all mixed up and confused. People lose their bearings and their moorings. That, says our Lord, is a period when sin abounds. And I do not hesitate to say that today we are living in just such a time: a time when sin is no longer a rivulet without menace or threat, but when sin and unbelief are threatening to carry away before them everything that you and I love; to sweep away everything precious, all that we believe in, and all the laws and practices that God has taught us in his word.

When sin abounds in this way, how are we to recognize the change? Let me give you some of the indications of it.

Our Lord refers in this sermon to persecution. He says that there will be a time when men will be cruel to one another. Parents will deliver up their children, and children their parents. You see the cruelty, the bitterness. There is a breakdown in families, a hostility and alienation between those who belong to the same family group. In some countries, it threatens to wipe out Christianity altogether.

As I speak today, Christians in Sudan are being taken away by the Muslim government authorities and being sold into slavery. Our beloved brethren in North Korea are suffering untold hardship and oppression, being threatened for their love of Jesus Christ. Some of them are, no doubt, being put in prison, in solitary confinement, and made to suffer all sorts of privations because of the love they bear to Christ.

This is a sign. Iniquity abounds and brings persecution; and you and I, if we know what lies ahead of us in the future, must prepare ourselves for any eventuality that may come to us in our lifetimes and in our own experience. We must make sure that we fortify our hearts by learning the doctrines of God's word and by filling ourselves with the knowledge of his truth, so that we may be prepared for any such evil day that may come to our own nations.

Another great evidence of when iniquity is abounding is the way in which morals decline in society and Christian influence almost vanishes. God is not mentioned any more in the classroom. No one thanks God for their food as once they used to do. There is no public recognition of the existence of God. A sort of confused atheism spreads over society. Men have no sense of the sinfulness of sin. Their consciences become hardened and deadened. They live for worldly things as though after death there were nothing to worry about, as though we are annihilated and vanish into nothingness. There is no sense of the importance of preparing to meet God. There is no fear of God. There is no desire to know God—no hungering and thirsting for righteousness.

Let me give you another evidence of it: when governments, to whom God has given authority to control crime and to put down evil, are instead weak and slack, and allow evil and crime to go unpunished. In these cases there is such pressure from godless men to do wicked things that the cry is heard everywhere, 'We have the right to do as we wish, the right to do what is wrong, what is vile, and to commit abominations and offend God with impunity.' So they think.

All of these marks and evidences are clearly things which we have come to see in our lifetime. Some of us, when we were young, never dreamed of the extent to which our societies would change. Things which were once said behind locked doors are now paraded in the headlines of newspapers and spoken about without shame in the media. It is a sign, as I say, of the fact that iniquity in society is abounding.

And all of this has an effect upon the Lord's people. Our Saviour is telling us that we are not immune from the influence of the world. Look at the way he puts it: he says that because iniquity shall abound, the result will be that love—the love of many Christians—will decline.

Why is that? One reason is because there is no more respect for Christians in society, and that is very hard for the Lord's people to bear, is it not? There was a day when godliness, decency, morality and the fear of God were held in estimation in society at large. Stability of character, stability in marriage and stability at work were things which were honoured and well spoken of. But in days like these, men turn truth upside down. They stand righteousness on its head, and they praise those who are unstable in character. They give honour to those who are unstable in marriage, unstable in outlook, unstable in work and unstable in their lifestyles. Everything is turned upside down, and the Lord's people are affected by the confusion. It is a sign that iniquity is abounding and that the wickedness of the age is having a harmful effect upon God's own people and their sanctification.

I believe it is no exaggeration to say that we are all deeply conscious of the spirit of the age in which we live. It is a spirit of fornication and adultery against God, a spirit of wickedness and of rebellion against heaven. It is a terrible thing when a footballer is worth £5 million but the souls of unborn children are worth nothing and are just so much rubbish to be carried away and burned in the incinerator.

Somebody put it like this: when the ship is in the water, that is good; but when the water is in the ship, that is harmful. When the church is in the world, that is good; but when the world is in the church, that is harmful. And that is the danger at such a time as this, because the people of God themselves become unclear. They lose their clear-cut witness to the things which their forefathers understood and believed. Do we not see this again and again in the book of Judges? The refrain that is repeated through the book is this: 'there was no king in Israel, but every man did that which was right in his own eyes' (Judg. 17:6). There was no norm, no standard. There was no clear grasp of God's word. There was no comprehension of the greatness or the glory of God. Truth had fallen in the street, and people were doing what was right in their own eyes because they knew no better; and the effect of it was that the people of God themselves were harmed by it.

We Christians are not an island. We are not insulated from society out there. We are all of us being influenced, pressurized, by the spirit of the age in which we live, and it is hurtful to our sanctification. It is a threat to our spirituality; and we see men fall, sometimes badly. Eminent Christians and eminent ministers are seen to drop over the horizon of fame. What has happened is that the sin of the age has swept them away. Iniquity abounds and it is a danger to the Lord's people—not just to one or two, you notice, but to 'many': 'Because iniquity shall abound, the love of many shall wax cold.' Our Lord tells us these things because we need these warnings. We need the preparation of heart to realize the dangers that such an age as this places us in. There is the danger that we could be carried away with the error of the wicked, that we could fail to hold fast to those foundations which are the very basis of our spiritual life and well-being.

What in particular, then, are the things that happen to the Lord's people who are called upon to live in an age of abounding wickedness like this present one? The first one is that they lose their love, says Christ. They lose their love, first of all, for Christ himself. One of the great casualties in the church when it is going through an abundantly sinful period is that heart-religion suffers.

In the great ages of the church the Lord's people cultivate their spiritual relationship with Christ himself. They believe in the religion of the heart, in having a warm heart. They come to conferences to have their hearts warmed, their memories stirred and their affections aroused by the recognition of the fact that Christ is with us still in our life on earth.

Whitefield spoke about having a 'felt' Christ. A 'felt' Christ is a Christ of whom we have much personal knowledge and with whom we have personal communion. The Bible talks about a 'joy unspeakable and full of glory', the 'peace of God, which passeth all understanding' and 'good hope through grace' (1 Pet. 1:8; Phil. 4:7; 2 Thess. 2:16). It talks about the wonderful love that exists between Christ and his people. It speaks of the Lord manifesting himself to us, Christ coming to us in our seasons of prayer and revealing himself to us so that our hearts truly burn within us. He communes with us, and this becomes our experience in this life.

But when iniquity is allowed to weaken the sanctification of our hearts and grace is in decline, the very first thing that happens to the people of God is that their love for Christ grows weak. They learn to be content to live without feelings. They simply go through the forms of religion without desiring their hearts to be moved and stirred by Christ's power. They become formalists. And it is possible for us to do this and not realize what is happening to us. We do not expect anything from God. The glories of the past are things of which we become utterly ignorant.

We refer to this technically as Sandemanianism. This is orthodox Christianity which is cold like an icicle. There is no warm love for Christ, no feeling for the things of God. Everything is done automatically. But Christ has something to say to us when we get into that state of soul. Remember how he put it to the Ephesian church: 'I have somewhat against thee, because thou hast left thy first love' (Eph. 2:4). Those words come to me personally as a most terrible indictment, more terrible than anything else that is written in Scripture. It is a most fearful thing for Christ to come to us and say, 'I have died for you, I have loved you with an everlasting love, but you have lost your love for me. You are too much in love with the world!'

I am afraid we see Christians today who have lost much of their love for Christ. How else do you explain all this love of the world, this love of entertainment, this love of pleasure which seems to be part of the life of modern Christians? How do you explain it except as a 'waxing cold'? Love has waxed cold because the pressure of this modern age is weakening the sanctification of God's people. It is, as it were, 'battering' against them. It is clamouring for attention. 'Oh!' says the conscience, 'I should spend time in secret prayer.' 'Nonsense!' says the world; 'you must watch this programme.' 'I must spend time with my Bible,' says my conscience. 'Not at all!' says the world; 'there is this worldly attraction that must be part of your daily schedule.' The people of God are caught in this conflict.

The way out is to see that we must please God alone in this life. We must learn to take up our cross and deny ourselves. We are to crucify our love of the world and to mortify our love of the things of this present age. We are to lust for nothing more than that we should live to the glory of God and the enjoyment of his presence with us in this life.

It is very sad to hear of the extent to which people who profess the Christian name can stretch the whole idea of Christian liberty. There is such a thing as Christian liberty. But we must never stretch it too far. We are free to do the will of God; we are not free to disobey the will of God. And that is something that I fear is being lost. I have met

Christians who seem to feel that it is quite safe for them to go to public houses and attend theatres and dances.

I feel very sad when I hear of professing Christians, and even sometimes ministers, who feel that they have the liberty to do these frivolous, trivial, unprofitable things. The Christian has no time for trivial pursuits; his aim is to get to heaven. Even the best Christian in this world has only one foot in heaven. You may say to me, 'I'm saved, I have come to Christ.' But you have only got one foot in heaven; you are not there yet. Make sure you get fully and entirely there. This demands that you should make every effort.

When love declines, our love for God's law declines, too. And that also is what has happened. There is in the world today something we refer to as 'Neo-Calvinism'. Some people are enthusiastic about reviewing theatres, films and the arts. They speak a good deal about the 'cultural mandate'. But they seem sometimes to have forgotten what we call the mandate to be holy: 'Be ye holy; for I am holy,' says the Lord (1 Pet. 1:16).

Another thing that suffers when the people of God are influenced by an abundantly evil generation is the worship of God. And, of course, we have seen this happening. Ever since the 1960s we have seen a tremendous decline in the quality of Christian worship. Our forefathers believed that we should come to the house of God after secret prayer and having prepared ourselves and had our souls moistened with the blessing of God. Then in God's house we should engage with concentration in prayer, in singing and in reading, and, above all, in listening to the preaching of the word of God.

But you do not need me to tell you that all over the world this has changed. Much 'worship' today consists in making as much noise as possible in the house of God. There is a loss of the sense of the holy presence of God, and that is because people have forgotten the principles of worship. 'Let us beware', says John Calvin, 'of disturbing pious minds by the introduction of any kind of novelty.' True biblical worship is sober, quiet, restrained, reverential, filled with holy fear and love for God.

But in days when iniquity abounds, all of this becomes unfashionable. People feel that they must entertain themselves, that they must turn the house of God into a place where there is mirth and frivolity. It is, I say, a turning of things upside down. But Jeremiah Burroughs, one of the Puritans, says in his famous book *Gospel Worship*, 'In matters of worship, God stands upon little things.' What does he mean by that? He means that as we come to God's house, God is very insistent that we do nothing in his own public worship except what we have a warrant for out of his own word. All that we do in the house of God, in other words, must have the warrant and authority of God's inspired word for it. That is to be the stamp, the hallmark, of our service to him in this world. But when iniquity abounds in society, the love of many waxes cold, and this is reflected in God's worship.

Are you keeping up your times of secret prayer from day to day? Are you reading your Bible consciously from day to day? You fathers, who are heads of families, are you conducting family worship from day to day, and teaching your family, leading them and setting them an example in the things of God? When your children and your wife look to you, do they say, 'Ah, there is a man of God'? Do they thank God that you are the head of their home, an example of what a Christian man, husband and father should be? Or are you being secretly influenced by the spirit of the age? Is the love of other things coming in so that you are growing cold? Is the world having upon you its harmful effect—the chilly, icy fingers of worldliness and compromise? Is it spoiling your family, your life, your church and your religion? Or are you aware of these evil things and resisting the devil?

You see how important it is in connection with our sanctification that we should value above all things our walk with God. We dare not lose it. We dare not sacrifice it for anything. We dare not allow the love of other things to come in and make the word of God unfruitful.

So, finally, let me point out to you that salvation will be given to everyone who perseveres in the faith until the end of their life. That is what my text informs us of: 'Because iniquity shall abound, the love of many shall wax cold. But he that shall endure unto the end, the same shall be saved.' So then, we are told, if we are the Lord's people and we mean business with God, we must endure. That means that we must endure hardness. You see the honesty of our Saviour. He does not tell us that the Christian life is easy, that to get to heaven will be easy. He says that to get to heaven is hard. It requires that we endure, that we persevere.

Every day we need to fight the good fight of faith and resist the powers of Satan. It is no easy matter to get to heaven. This world was a great trial for Christ. It was a most evil world, a world of sorrows, for him. It is no wonder that he is said in Scripture to be 'a man of sorrows, and acquainted with grief' (Isa. 53:3). And it is like that in a measure for every one of the children of God. It is a hard world and a hard fight, and it requires that we watch in case we should be squeezed into the world's mould. We must constantly watch for anything which might eat up our spiritual life and damage our soul and our sanctification.

Persevering means, first of all, that we endure in our love for the word of God. We are to love the Bible, the whole Bible. This is the sum and substance of our religion. We must never let anyone filch from us our confidence in the word of God. The Bible, the whole Bible and nothing but the Bible, is our true and sure foundation. When the love of Christians begins to wax weak and cold, they lose their assurance of what the Bible is. But we must not allow that to happen. Perseverance means that we endure in our certainty that every word of the Bible in the original languages is fully reliable. The Old Testament in Hebrew and

Aramaic and the New Testament in Greek were verbally inspired and are absolutely trustworthy. And we believe that our good old English version is a reliable translation of the word of God.

Worldly influences today pressurize us to lose faith in the Bible. The world—the media, the press, the academic world—are all pressurizing us to move away from this certainty. But we are to persevere in our absolute certainty that what God has said will stand. Notice how Christ puts this: he says, 'Heaven and earth shall pass away, but my words shall not pass away' (Matt. 24:35). What a statement! What an assurance! The world would love to take away our confidence in the message of the gospel. But we must not be ashamed of the testimony of the Lord or of the gospel, which is the power of God.

Next, we are to persevere in our adherence to the good old theology of our forefathers. We are to believe in the Westminster Confession of Faith and the catechisms. We are to believe that they are the sum and substance of the doctrine of the word of God. We are not to let anyone undermine our certainty that those old truths are revealed by God. They are the body of divinity which heaven has revealed for the edification, strengthening and upbuilding of the people of God until the end shall come.

Theology does not change any more than mathematics changes. Two plus two equalled four in the days of Adam, and they will equal four in the days when the trumpet sounds at the end of time. So with theology. We need not apologize for being 'old fashioned' in that sense. When people say that we are believing yesterday's gospel, we say, 'Amen!' It is yesterday's and tomorrow's gospel—one gospel, one theology. We do not apologize. We persevere in it in spite of the derision of men, in spite of the contempt of the academic world. We know that this is the religion of God.

In addition, we are to persevere in offering free salvation to men and women through faith alone in Christ. We are to tell them that God will receive penitent sinners no matter how wicked, how sinful, they are. God welcomes the penitent sinner. 'Come,' says God, 'for all things are now ready' (Luke 14:17) . He brings home the sinner who puts his trust in Jesus, be he never so vile in his past life. If his heart is broken to repentance, God will have him and receive him gladly.

Finally, we are to persevere in waiting patiently for the coming of the Lord. It is a hard thing to wait for Christ's return. The church in every age has cried, 'Even so, come, Lord Jesus.' But Christ is waiting, and keeping us waiting, until all his elect from the four corners of the earth are brought in. He mentions that in a similar chapter. The saved of all nations and all ages will come 'from the east, and from the west, and from the north, and from the south' (Luke 13:29). He will bring all his people home at last through the preaching of the truth. And when the last of his blood-bought children has come in, time shall be no longer. The angel will put his trumpet to his lips, heaven and earth will pass away, and all things will be fulfilled.

We are called upon as Christians to suffer in this world for a little time. Don't try to remove from your Christian life the element of suffering; it is ordained by God. Suffering here will make heaven sweeter hereafter. This world is not our home. But we do have a home. It is a house of many mansions which Christ is now preparing for us. This world is but the 'gymnasium' in which we are being exercised, but that world is the haven of rest in which we shall glory eternally in the love of God and experience the floods of that love poured out upon our souls.

In heaven we shall see the glory of the Father, Son and Holy Spirit. We shall wake up satisfied with the likeness of God. We shall be like Christ: he will be the firstborn among many brethren, and we will be conformed perfectly to his image. There we shall enjoy heaven as a world of love. Eternal glories will be at the right hand of God. They will make up for all the sufferings of God's people here in this life.

But we must watch in case the spirit of the world should come in; in case the subtle suggestions of the devil should weaken our resolve and our desire to persevere to the end. How true this text is! Iniquity in some ages does abound. And how sadly true it is to observe that, because iniquity abounds, the love of many Christians grows cold! But you and I, hearing these things, must cry to God afresh today and say, 'Lord, fill us with thy truth, fill us with thy Holy Spirit, fill us with a holy energy so that we might spend all our days in this present age wrestling against the powers of the devil. We know that when the age is over and the end shall come we will rest eternally with thee, world without end. Amen.'

TWO

Praying in the Spirit

> *Likewise the Spirit also helpeth our infirmities: for we know not what we should pray for as we ought: but the Spirit itself maketh intercession for us with groanings which cannot be uttered. And he that searcheth the hearts knoweth what is the mind of the Spirit, because he maketh intercession for the saints according to the will of God.*—Rom. 8:26, 27.

The subject which is before us is that of praying in the Spirit. I suggest that this is a most essential element of the sanctifying work of the Spirit of God in the hearts and lives of his people here in this life. Prayer is essential if you and I are to go to heaven. None ever got to heaven who did not pray. And it is ordained by God that so long as we are in the body we must continue instant in prayer, with all prayer and supplication in the Spirit. The reason for that is because in the life of grace, God has ordained that nothing should be automatic. The grace which we receive, we are given largely in answer to prayer. This is therefore the way in which the Lord sanctifies his people. The measure of grace we have is very closely connected to the measure of our prayerfulness. The more prayerful we are, the more spiritual we shall tend to be.

I must say that all my life, as a Christian believer and as a minister, I have found prayer difficult. It is not that it is unwelcome: there is nothing more profitable, nothing more delightful, than to hold communion with God. But I cannot pretend that prayer is easy.

But our text tells us something that should encourage us. At verse 26 the Apostle Paul informs us that we do not know what we should pray for as we ought. And from those words I draw out this point of doctrine: that the believer finds prayer difficult, and that it should not surprise the believer if that is so.

You will meet people who will say to you that prayer is easy. They will say that there is nothing to prayer but simply saying a few words to Jesus. We must not despise those who talk in this way, but if saying 'a few words to Jesus' is all that prayer is, I doubt very much if the Apostle Paul would have written this text at all.

I believe that prayer, when it is prayer in the Spirit, is something which is an experience. I shall come back to this later, but I mention the point now that when prayer is in the Spirit of God it is not simply an utterance of words by us; it is an experience of the Spirit of God in our hearts. How do I know? Because Paul tells us so at the end of verse 26: 'The Spirit itself maketh intercession for us with groanings which cannot be uttered.' I would argue that you cannot have 'groanings' without having an experience. When a man groans, it is because he is deeply conscious of some inward pain or anguish which draws out of him a sigh or a moan. That is an experience. I would therefore argue that one of the most sanctifying experiences which we can have today is this prayer in the Spirit of which the apostle is speaking.

We must begin by saying that the believer must expect to find prayer difficult: 'We know not what we should pray for as we ought.' If any Christian has never experienced difficulty in prayer, I suggest it is because he knows very little about what real praying is. We begin to learn about prayer when we learn how difficult prayer can be. The Apostle Paul, then, is saying something which is true of all believers, and it is true even of himself. He is not saying that others find praying difficult; he says that 'we' find it difficult. Even the Apostle Paul, when he came to pray, found prayer difficult.

We would often have to echo the same sentiment, would we not? We scarcely know with what words to address God. This is true of secret prayer in the closet, family prayer and public prayer. It is a very humbling fact. There are days when we find prayer intensely hard. Not every day: some days you go into the closet and you pray, and as you are praying you get help, you get liberty—and I will speak about that in a moment. But there are other days when your soul is wooden and you feel that there is no wing to lift you into an airborne condition. You feel your prayer hardly gets off the ground. The Apostle Paul was no doubt acquainted with that problem.

Why do we find prayer so difficult? Partly it is because sin has ruined us all. Sin has had such an effect upon us that we are no longer men but simply the 'rubbish' of a man, as someone once put it. That is all that is left of us. Sin has un-manned us. It has ruined us, and consequently we find it very hard to engage in a spiritual exercise. To address the Almighty God is certainly a deeply spiritual exercise.

But what precisely is the difficulty about prayer? Here I will first say what it is *not*. The difficulty in prayer is not simply the *manner* in which we pray. By that I mean the choice of good words. There is a place in prayer for the choice of suitable language and diction, and I will put in a plea for the old Authorized Version because there is no better source of beautiful language than this great old version of the Bible. It is a well of English undefiled, and those who study it will find themselves well supplied with spiritual language with which to address God.

But that is not the whole problem. It is not simply a question of the manner with which we come before God. I can prove that easily because the scribes and the Pharisees were no doubt excellent in the use of language; but their prayers were not acceptable to God.

Secondly, it is not just the way in which we use our voice. This is an interesting subject, is it not? When people pray they change their voice. I am not going to say that that is altogether wrong, but I do suggest that it may not altogether be right. We must be careful that we do not develop an artificiality of voice in prayer. I knew an old Scottish minister, now in glory, who said something to me once which was so surprising and arresting I never forgot it: 'If you were to drop me blindfold into any church in the Highlands of Scotland not knowing the denomination, as soon as I heard the people pray I could tell you at once what their denomination was!' He would know if they were Church of Scotland, Free Presbyterian, and so forth. How would he know? By the way they used their voice! This is something in which we have to be self-critical.

C. H. Spurgeon put it in a rather memorable phrase: he talked about the 'steeple-in-the-throat'-sort of voice in which people put on an oily, unctuous sound. I am not saying that that is altogether and always out of place; there is a way in which the voice is going to be affected by our very reverence. But here I am simply saying that that is not the main problem which is set before us by the Apostle Paul.

What, then, is the difficulty? The difficulty is that when I am face-to-face with God, what do I say? There, I believe, is the problem. We are, as it were, embarrassed before God and we find it hard to know how to address his divine Majesty. With what words, with what sentiments, with what requests, do I lift up my heart to the great and glorious Creator of heaven and earth, our heavenly Father?

There are times, I think, when we would almost die rather than pray. This is one reason why the Christian must keep himself from foolishness of mind, frivolity of heart and worldliness of disposition. If you allow yourself to drift into worldly thoughts, worldly interests and worldly occupations beyond what is legitimate, it will make it so much harder for you to address God. I believe you know from experience that this is so.

This is an important subject because, of course, there is too little spiritual praying in this world, and it is a world that greatly needs much prayer. Our nations need much prayer from the Lord's people. It is our duty to bring affairs of church and state, personal matters, family matters and church matters before God. This is our great privilege and honour. To be praying, therefore, in the Spirit for all aspects of the life of our church and nation is of great benefit to both church and state. Some of the most important people in any country today are those who are praying for the good of the land. They may not get into the headlines, and they may not be spoken about over the radio or on television, but if men had eyes to see who a nation's true friends are they would see that they are those Christians who pray for their beloved and precious land.

I saw a poster in Inverness just a few days ago from one of the political parties. It was saying to the people of Scotland, 'Scotland, get off your knees!' The impression was that Scotland was like a subject nation and we ought to get off our knees and fight for our rights. What a sad reflection of the ignorance of our day! If they knew the message Scotland needed, it would be 'Scotland, get back *on* your knees', because that is where very great good is done. I do not think I am exaggerating when I say that as sanctification declines, so does this gift of spiritual prayer.

An experience I had some years ago in Cornwall serves to illustrate this. Cornwall is right at the south-west tip of England, and the gospel came to it especially through the Methodists. I had been preaching on the subject of prayer in a certain church there, and when I had finished I went to the front door to shake hands with those who had been present. Amongst them was an elderly man who, as he shook my hand, said to me, 'Young man, when I was a young Christian in the 1920s we would go to the old Methodist prayer meetings, and there we would have our meetings mid-week for prayer. The old men used to go down on their knees on the bare boards and they would plead with God for the blessing to come down. You would feel the difference. You would feel the heavenly influence coming into the gathering.' Then he added, 'There's *nobody* prays like that any more. Nobody *can* pray like that any more.'

I laid that to my heart and it made me realize once again that prayer is the thermometer of the soul, and if we are to excel in prayer, we have got to excel in sanctification; we have got to excel in spirituality; we have got to excel in the knowledge of God. No man can pray with all the energies of his soul or pour himself out, as it were, before God unless and until he lives close to God. He must live in the secret place of the Most High and under the shadow of the Almighty.

In the great days of old some of our eminent forefathers were outstanding examples in prayer. John Knox, the great Scottish Reformer, was an eminent man of prayer. Mary, Queen of Scots admitted that she feared the prayers of John Knox more than an army of soldiers coming expressly against the kingdom. She knew that this man's prayers made a great difference in the nation. The same can be said of the prayers of Martin Luther in Germany at the time of the Reformation. He so interceded with God that Melanchthon, who had been very ill, was raised up again to continue the great work of Reformation with him.

These things are not legends; they are not mythical. They show what spiritual praying can do. It was said of the minister John Welsh of Ayr in Scotland, son-in-law of John Knox, that he often prayed for eight hours a day. He would intercede for the protection of the land from the forces of evil that were invading and trying to destroy the gospel. One night, he got up from his bed to plead for Scotland. His wife heard him praying like this: 'Give me Scotland; O God, give me Scotland.' You see the mystery associated with these men. They were mighty men in prayer.

I have argued, then, that prayer is difficult. Remember

that when even our Saviour Jesus Christ was in the garden of Gethsemane, he lay flat upon the ground and his sweat as he prayed was like great drops of blood. The Scripture says about Christ, 'He prayed', and then, 'He prayed *more earnestly*' (Luke 22:44). Think about that: even Christ could pray at different levels of earnestness. And so can we. I believe that we should stir ourselves up sometimes to pray with very special urgency. Close the doors and make sure that nobody is listening. Get on your own, lift up your voice and cry to high heaven with all the energies of your soul that God would visit us again, that he would come down and bless his cause and make the preaching of the gospel an engine for bringing sinners out of their darkness and into the marvellous light of the gospel.

Then, secondly, having told us that prayer is difficult, the Apostle Paul gives us further encouragement: 'The Spirit also helpeth our infirmities.' Of course, we are to help ourselves in prayer. One way to do this is to learn the Bible. Learn as much of this blessed Book as you can. Men may scoff at the Bible or think little of it today, but it is the way to become mighty in prayer. Those who know this Book well will be men and women of prayer.

Another thing we can do to help ourselves in prayer is study to obey God carefully. Walk and live by the rule of his word and keep a good conscience. No man can pray with closeness or earnestness if he has a bad conscience. This is why we must keep our conscience clear and cleansed by the blood of Christ. A cleansed conscience is the best preparative for holding communion with God.

But more than all this, we must plead with God to send upon us the influences of his Holy Spirit. That is especially what Paul is referring to here. The help which God has provided for us in prayer is help given by the Holy Spirit.

Men have found many false and wrong ways of helping themselves in prayer. It is a proof of the difficulty that people have in prayer that they have invented all sorts of ways of getting around the problem. The worst of all these is the rosary—a string of beads which the Roman Catholic Church gives to people who, instead of uttering words of prayer to God, are told that they simply need to touch each of these beads and say, 'Hail Mary, Mother of God, remember me now and when I die', or words to that effect. They finger these beads and think that by so doing they are praying to God. What is wrong with that? It is treating God like a machine: 'If I do this, I want that in exchange.' It is like when you put in a coin, pull a lever, and then out comes the bar of chocolate. That is an abomination with God. God is a holy Person with a free will, and if we treat him like a machine we shall offend him and grieve his Spirit.

Another dangerous method of prayer is the prayer book. I am not saying that it is always wrong to read prayers from a prayer book. Fluent speech is very important in prayer and can be helpful. Some prayers are very edifying; some people's prayers are beautiful. But real prayer begins with the heart and expresses itself through the lips to God. If you have a prayer book, however, it is the book that is leading the heart. What is God looking at in prayer? Is he looking at our lips? Is he looking at our powers of reading? No, he is looking at our hearts, the state of our souls and the sincerity of our asking. It is our faith in Christ and our confidence in his Fatherly goodness and gracious promises to do us good that he regards. So there is a danger attached to using a prayer book. It is like living all your life as a cripple when you have two healthy legs to walk on. You would say of a man who did that, that he was ruining his own life. If we are dependent on any external aid like a prayer book we are running this danger. Books of prayer are not to be relied upon as the real method of uttering our prayers to God. The soul must lead the words, not the words the soul.

So what is the essence of prayer? It is very hard to say what the essence of prayer is, but when you hear a man who *really* is in prayer, you know at once that he is holding communion with God. I cannot say how you know, but you *do* know. You feel it; you are arrested and gripped by it.

An experience I had once in Glasgow illustrates this. I went to a presbytery prayer meeting held by the Free Church of Scotland. All the churches in the presbytery gathered for it—perhaps 150 people, gathered for prayer. I was called on by the minister to pray, and I prayed a rather stiff and ordinary prayer and sat down disappointed. Others then prayed in the same sort of way. I must confess that I began to lose my concentration. But then the minister called upon a man to pray who at that time was a stranger to me.

I had never heard this man before and had never met him in my life, but when I heard him pray I rejoiced that there were still persons in Glasgow who could pray like that man. He was wrestling with God. He knew God intimately. He knew how to address him. He knew how to call upon him. His soul was pouring out wondrous intercessions and uttering urgent petitions. When we sat down after that man's prayer I felt renewed and refreshed. That was the wonderful thing.

The difference was this: I and others had prayed without much of the Spirit in our souls. But when *that* man prayed, his whole soul was glowing with the Spirit of God. There was a sort of incandescence within him—and we felt it, and we felt the better for it. I suppose I will never forget this experience as long as I live. And that, I believe, is what the Apostle Paul is speaking about: '*The Spirit helpeth* our infirmities.' We do not know what to pray for; we find it so hard to address God. But God has given us this wonderful help. It is not simply fluency of speech; God has given us this influence of the Holy Spirit upon our spirit. That is the way we are to look at it, I believe. 'He maketh intercession for the saints according to the will of God.'

Notice that, in prayer, when it is real prayer, there are, quite apart from ourselves, two intercessors. There is an external intercessor at the right hand of God. That is, of course, Christ. Christ is making intercession at the r hand of God. But also there is this other intercessor— Spirit of God himself who is in our hearts. He is creating prayer, he is stirring up the soul with the desire to pray. And that is called the Spirit's interceding.

How are we to understand the Spirit's intercession? I think we should be very careful about the way we define it. The Spirit of God is not praying outside us, but inside us. Christ is praying outside us; he is above as the intercessor with the Father. But the Holy Spirit is praying within us; he is stirring us up. The best illustration I can think of is that of a harpist. You know, perhaps, of those wonderful Welsh harps—what beautiful instruments they are! The harpist comes and sits beside the harp and the whole instrument becomes alive. That is what the Spirit of God does: he fires the soul; he touches the emotions; he brings the melody of the heart out; and the music begins to ascend. It is the music of the soul, the love of the soul for God, the yearning of the heart after God. Is this not what the psalmist tells us in Psalm 42:1: 'As the hart panteth after the water brooks, so panteth my soul after thee, O God'? The Spirit of God is poured out upon the heart and he makes intercession for the saints according to the will of God.

We do not always pray like that, but we should strive to pray like that every day. We should strive to pray in such a manner that we have emotion, feeling, desire and ardour for God. We should not be disappointed or surprised if we have tears running down our face before we are finished. That is to be desired. We need to have a desire after God himself.

There is nothing I know of that is more sanctifying, more conducive to holiness, than this experience of prayer in the Spirit. I am inclined to think that there are two kinds of prayer. There is prayer, and there is prayer in the Spirit. You may say to me, 'What's the difference?' Let me make it very clear that when I speak of prayer in the Spirit, I am not referring to speaking with tongues, prophecy, signs or wonders, or anything of that kind. What I believe Paul is talking about is the influence of the Holy Spirit upon our spirits and the touch of God's divine grace upon our hearts giving us a sense of love for God. It has nothing at all to do with signs and wonders. It has everything to do with communion with God.

Paul puts it that way in Ephesians 6:18: 'praying always with all prayer and supplication in the Spirit'. Is not that interesting? We are not just to pray, but to pray 'in the Spirit'. I believe that is connected with this whole subject before us. We are to expect that when we pray we shall be helped. Sometimes we pray and we are not helped; we have to do it all ourselves. But there are times when we pray and we do not do it all ourselves; we are aware that our hearts are led out and our souls are enlarged, sometimes far beyond what we imagine. And there are times when we go on our knees and we feel wooden. Then, as we wait on God, our souls are moistened and our hearts softened, and we suddenly discover that we can cry out with warmth and familiarity to God. When we have finished we know that we have had communion with the Almighty; we have had dealings with heaven. That, I think, is what Paul is referring to here: 'The Spirit also helpeth our infirmities.'

It is in place to look at this word 'helpeth' and to say something about its original meaning in the Greek. Charles Hodge comments, 'This word means, to take hold of anything with another, to take part of his burden or work.' John Calvin's commentary on this word is, 'The Spirit takes part of the burden with which our weakness is weighed down.'

The following illustration may help us understand what is being talked about here. Imagine there is a large plank of wood in a room. Into the room comes a little boy followed by his father. The boy knows that his father intends to move the plank, so, being a boy, he wants to try his strength and see if he can lift it himself. The little fellow goes to one end and he manages to raise the plank six inches. His father smiles and goes to the other end, and, with his brawny arms, he lifts the whole plank with the boy still holding on. The father smiles again and says, 'Well done, boy! We'll carry this together.' And of course the boy is delighted, not realizing that almost the entire weight is resting with the father, and all that he is doing is putting his fingertips to it. Both of them are taking the burden!

That is similar to what this word implies in the original Greek language. Two are taking one burden. In the case of prayer, it is the Spirit of God taking the burden with the Christian. The Spirit helps us in this great task.

Prayer is a burden. I do not know what you pray for, but I feel we must pray for all the world. Where do you begin? I begin in my own country. I always go on to Israel and to the Jews, then I go all around the world, including the Middle East, Africa, America, Australia, New Zealand, and so on. They are all precious countries. They are countries where God has a people and a work to be done. We are called upon to bear this burden more or less every day we live. We pray too for our families, our congregations and our society. All of these things are fit subjects for prayer.

What a burden! Who can live carrying such a burden day after day? How are we to carry it? Well, says Paul, you are not on your own. There is another one carrying the burden with you. 'The Spirit helpeth our infirmities.' That is the comfort we have. In prayer there is not just one person but there are two persons who are active together. Real prayer involves two, not one. It is God the Spirit helping us, his people, to carry the burden of the cause of Christ upon earth, to present to God the responsible burdens which we share and carry in life, 'casting all [our] care upon him, for he careth for [us]' (1 Pet. 5:7), rolling our burden upon the Lord because it is too heavy for us, '[being] careful for nothing, but in every thing by prayer and supplication with thanksgiving [letting our] requests be made known unto God' (Phil. 4:6).

There are times, I think, when we should compare prayer to a millstone grinding the wheat. In the old days, wheat was ground between two millstones. We used to speak of the upper millstone and the nether, or lower, millstone. These two millstones were the means of grinding the wheat into flour. The lower millstone was stationary and the upper millstone was turned with a handle. So, in prayer, we are ground out like wheat. The lower millstone is the promise of God and the upper millstone is the providence of God. As we look about us in this world, we see what appears to be a contradiction between what God has promised to do and what in his providence he does do. We see a sort of conflict between the promise and the providence.

You see this all the way through the Psalms. Take Psalm 44. 'O God,' says the psalmist, 'our fathers have told us, what work thou didst in their days, in the times of old. How thou didst drive out the heathen with thy hand', and so forth. Then he says, 'But it is not happening in our days. The day was when thy power was visible. But this is not so any more. We are a laughing-stock to our neighbours. The name of God is trampled upon, truth is despised, the word is hated.' What he is doing is using the promise as the basis for his pleadings. He sees the providence apparently in contradiction to the promise and this grinds the fine meal and the fine wheat of true spiritual prayer.

I must add that this is an experience. Real prayer is an experience! How do I know? Because, as I said before, the

Apostle Paul speaks of 'groanings'—'groanings which cannot be uttered'. They are inexpressible, ineffable. You cannot put into words some of the things you yearn to say to God. There are some prayer meetings where there is a great deal of noise during the prayer time. Some people are grunting and groaning and uttering words, and they think that that is the expression of God's Spirit. But the interesting thing is that this apostolic type of prayer has groanings that cannot be uttered! You cannot hear the groanings. Real prayer groans in the heart, not in the vocal chords. It is something that is going on in the secret places, in the very bowels, of a man's soul. He is burdened for the cause of God, and that is what he expresses. I spoke earlier about Luther's prayers, but maybe you have had these experiences yourself. This intense type of prayer goes beyond words. It is a profound desire to say things to God which are beyond our own powers of expression. And we are helped by the Spirit to utter these desires.

I must come to my final point. You may say to me, 'How will I know when I am truly praying in the Spirit with these experiences of groaning? How will I know when I am praying as I should?' Let me give you four evidences, as I see it, of what I call 'praying in the Spirit'—ways whereby we may recognize when we pray in the Spirit.

The first is this: if you go into your closet and, after prayer, discover that you had forgotten everything in the world, I would say that there is proof that you were praying in the Spirit. I suggest that in this type of prayer you forget yourself, your problems and the things in your life, and when you come out of the time of prayer you realize that you were in a 'different world' for a while. I would say without doubt that when you have this feeling you have been helped by the Spirit of God, because all too often our minds are full of ourselves, our problems and our world, and we do not get beyond that. But when the Spirit helps us, we forget these other things for a time.

The second evidence that you have prayed in the Spirit is if you know that you are not on your own in prayer. When you have the heart-warming feeling that Christ is with you and beside you, and that he is truly hearing and helping, then I say you have another evidence that the Spirit has helped you.

A third test is this: when you have a feeling of inward constraint. From time to time we get that. You do not know why, but there is a burden that comes upon you, a conscious desire to get away and be apart with God. When that happens I say you must regard it as a sign that you are being helped in prayer. As far as you possibly can, always yield to that and find a quiet place. God is constraining you to prayer.

But, most wonderfully of all, I believe that there is a further sign that we have been helped in prayer: it is when, after we have prayed, our soul is amazed and we can say to ourselves that we had extraordinary fluency, freedom and earnestness. Let me give an illustration of this.

In 1859 there was a revival in Scotland. It had begun in New York and came to Northern Ireland and then to Scotland, England, Ireland and Wales. There was a tremendous blessing in Britain, America and elsewhere at that time.

In a town in Ayrshire in south-west Scotland there was a school room where a religious meeting was being held. The Spirit of God was working so powerfully that the people would not go home after the meeting. Sinners were in tears all round the room and they were being counselled by their Christian friends. Christians were trying to help them to find Christ, and they would not go home.

The minister was watching all this. Some were rejoicing in sins forgiven, and others were burdened because they had not received assurance. Others, as I say, were under conviction of sin. The minister watched the meeting going on and on for hour after hour, and still the people would not go home. Eventually he stood up and felt it his duty to dismiss the people in case they were exhausted the next day. He said to them, 'Friends, you've got to go home. I am going to pray before you go.' So he prayed. He prayed that night as he had never prayed before! Afterwards, he said, 'What a prayer!'

This, I firmly believe, is the evidence that he was praying with extraordinary help from God. I believe I am warranted to say that we shall all find it a profoundly sanctifying and solemnizing experience of the grace of God to pray like this.

May God teach us all to pray indeed 'in the Spirit'!

THREE

The Start of Sanctification

For ye have not received the spirit of bondage again to fear; but ye have received the Spirit of adoption, whereby we cry, Abba, Father. The Spirit itself beareth witness with our spirit, that we are the children of God.—Rom. 8:15, 16.

The particular subject which comes to our attention now is that of the start of sanctification. How does sanctification begin? That is an important question because human nature is very unsanctified. It is not simply that men do not love God, but men hate him. It is not simply that our willpower is somewhat disinclined to obey God; the truth of the matter is that the will of man is entirely opposed to the will of God. We resist the operations of God's grace and Spirit. We withstand his truth and contradict his voice all through our lives unless by grace we come to faith in Christ.

So the start of the work of sanctification is a wonderful subject in itself. It commands our attention. It is one of the greatest wonders of the world that God can bring a clean thing out of an unclean. Indeed, in the moral sphere it is nothing less than a stupendous miracle that men and women who are half beast and half devil can become partakers of the divine nature and obedient children of God, conforming to the image of his will and preparing for the glory of God beyond the grave, for this is the Christian's destiny.

The words of our text give us a wonderful entrance into the subject of how sanctification begins. I propose to look at the subject under the natural headings suggested by the way Paul has written down the doctrines here. First of all, we shall look at what is meant by the spirit of bondage. Later, we will also look at the Spirit of adoption. But between these two—the spirit of bondage and the Spirit of adoption—occurs the new birth. So, secondly, we shall look at the new birth.

In the course of looking at these subjects we shall, I believe, come to understand how the work of grace begins within the soul. The great theme before us, then, is this: God begins to make men and women his own dear children and cleanses human nature, purifies their hearts and prepares them for glory and eternal rest.

We notice first of all, then, that Paul speaks of the 'spirit of bondage'. He tells the Roman Christians here that they had once upon a time received this spirit of bondage to fear. Notice that word 'again': it means that they did receive it once, at some time in the past, but they have not received it again. We are forced to enquire, then, what does the apostle mean when he talks about the spirit of bondage?

There are excellent commentators who understand that

by this expression 'the spirit of bondage' Paul is referring to the condition of men before their conversion. They say that all men are under God's law, are condemned because of sin, and before their conversion are slaves of sin and so are in a state of bondage. That is the way it is explained by Hodge and by Haldane, I believe. They take the spirit of bondage here not to be the Holy Spirit, but that attitude of mind which is typical of unconverted men and women.

This view is true as far as it goes. But I do not believe that that is exactly what the Apostle Paul means here. I feel convinced that Paul is referring to the Holy Spirit and not simply to the general spirit of the world or the condition or mentality of men and women without God. It is certainly true that men and women without God are in bondage and are slaves of sin. Ungodly men are afraid in case the Christian faith is correct and there is a hell and a judgment day when they have to meet their Maker. The natural man has many fears of that kind.

But the distinct thing that the apostle is teaching, I believe, is this: that the Holy Spirit operates and works upon the hearts of men in such a way as to cause in them, before conversion, a special kind of fear.

You will notice that all through Romans 8 there are repeated references to the Holy Spirit. Take, for instance, Romans 8:4. Paul talks about walking after the Spirit, meaning that the Christian lives his life according to the teaching of the Spirit in the Bible. In verse 5 he talks about those who mind the things of the Spirit. A little further down he speaks about the work of the Holy Spirit in the sense of giving us the mind of the Spirit. And in verse 9 he says that the Spirit of God dwells in the Christian; the Holy Spirit resides in his heart. Go down to verse 11 and you see that the Spirit is said to raise up the Christian from the dead on the resurrection day. And then we come to verse 14: the Christian is 'led by the Spirit'. These verses indicate that all through this passage the apostle is talking about the operations and activities of the Holy Spirit within the heart and life of a believer. So there is good reason, I think, to believe that in verse 15, when he speaks about the spirit of bondage, he is speaking about the Holy Spirit.

Do not be misled or confused by the fact that there is only a lower-case 's' here. The original Greek language had neither upper-case nor lower-case letters. So it is a matter of editorial decision as to whether you print the word with a capital letter or not. And there is reason to believe that, since Paul is talking about the Holy Spirit all through this passage, he is also referring in both parts of verse 15 to the work and activity of the Holy Spirit.

What, then, is this doctrine? Surely it is this: that before the conversion of a man to faith in Christ there is a distinct operation of the Holy Spirit whereby he is made to have fear. This fear is a realization by the sinner that God exists. It is a wholesome work of the Spirit upon his conscience to make him realize that he must get right with God.

That is the nature of the Spirit's work as it is defined by the Apostle Paul here. He refers to this as the Spirit 'of bondage' because it brings a sinner to recognize his bondage, to realize that he is a captive and under the power of sin. It makes him realize that he cannot escape from God. The Spirit of bondage is a preparatory work of the Holy Spirit whereby God touches the heart of a sinner and prepares him for faith in the Lord Jesus Christ by impressing upon him that he is in prison, ripe for judgment, under condemnation and under the curse of God.

Sinners do not ordinarily think of themselves in that way. They think of themselves as free. They never dream that they are slaves to sin and Satan. A man who is without Christ regards himself as much freer than the Christian. He congratulates himself that he is free to go anywhere. He can go to clubs, public houses, entertainment places and nightclubs without any fear of anything—so he thinks. He pities men and women like you and me who spend time in church buildings. He regards us as slaves to some sort of religious obsession, and himself as free.

But what he does not know is that as a sinner he is under the bondage of sin, and he will never know that until God the Holy Spirit acts upon his mind, heart and conscience so as to convince him of his true condition. That, I believe, is what is referred to here as 'the Spirit of bondage'.

There are very important passages of Scripture that deal with this theme. Take, for instance, the words of our Saviour in John 16:8: 'When he is come, he will reprove the world of sin, and of righteousness, and of judgment.' That is, of course, a reference to the Holy Spirit, and our Saviour is telling us that the distinct ministry of the Holy Spirit when he comes after Pentecost will be to go into the world and to show men their genuine condition. He will bring home to them the sinfulness of their lives, that they are under the condemnation of the Moral Law. He will convince the world of sin, righteousness and judgment. This is the same teaching that we have in Romans 8:15.

Romans 7:7–13 is also closely related to our text. First, I need to say something about Romans 7 as a whole. Romans 7:1–6, the first section of the chapter, deals with the change which occurs in the life of a believer from being married to the Moral Law to being married to Christ. This is a most important passage of Scripture and one that deserves to be most carefully studied. In Romans 7:14–25, the third section of the chapter, the apostle talks about the problem of the Christian's indwelling sin. The Christian who has been justified and in whom the Spirit of God dwells still has this problem of indwelling sin.

However, my present concern is with the middle passage of the chapter, Romans 7:7–13. Here you notice that the Apostle Paul is talking about himself. He relates an experience of his own past life: 'I had not known sin, but by the law.' He says, in effect, 'I was once upon a time confident that I had kept God's Moral Law—the ten commandments. I was certain that I was a righteous man. The basis of my certainty and confidence was that I kept God's law as scrupulously as I knew how. I was a Pharisee of the Pharisees, one of the strictest, and I supposed as a Pharisee that, because I was strict and conscientious in keeping the moral requirements of God, I was in a good relationship with my Maker and I was going to heaven. But then,' he says, 'something happened to me.' He describes this in verses 7 to 13. What was it?

He says, 'The commandment came … and I died.' Which commandment came? He is quite clear: it was the commandment which says 'Thou shalt not covet'. Then he says in verse 8: 'Sin, taking occasion by the commandment, wrought in me all manner of concupiscence.' Concupiscence means lust, or sin. So at a crucial point in his life as a proud Pharisee he suddenly realized that the tenth commandment requires of men that they do not even *desire* what is evil. That was a new thought to him. It is one thing not to commit adultery, not to steal and not to kill. That is right and good as far as it goes. But the tenth commandment forbids us even to be lustful. We are not even to have an evil *thought*. That too is sin against God.

It was the Holy Spirit who brought this tenth commandment home to Paul's conscience, and he puts it in a very interesting way: 'when the commandment came, sin revived, and I died.' This is his way of saying, 'I came to see that I was not righteous before God, but a lost sinner. All my confidence as a Pharisee was punctured; all my self-assurance and self-righteousness received a mighty blow. How? Because the Holy Spirit of God, taking the tenth commandment and revealing to me the requirement of God to be pure in heart as well as in the body, convinced me that I was guilty after all I had done!' And he was devastated.

So you could say that here in Romans 7:7–13 Paul is talking about the first beginnings of his conversion. We have the story of his conversion told in Acts 9 and on certain other occasions in the Acts of the Apostles where he gives his testimony. We know the outward events of that conversion. He was travelling on the road to Damascus when suddenly a light shone about him, brighter than the noonday sun, and he fell down to the ground. Christ said to him, 'Saul, Saul, why persecutest thou me?' And he said, 'Who art thou, Lord?' The voice replied, 'I am Jesus whom thou persecutest: it is hard for thee to kick against the pricks' (Acts 9:4–5).

Evidently Paul had been resisting certain qualms of conscience. Even before he saw the glory of Christ, the Spirit of God had begun to prepare him for that conversion, by pricking his conscience.

These pricks of conscience are precisely what we have in our text in Romans 8:15 where the Spirit of God is said to be a Spirit of bondage and to bring the sinner to fear because of his condition. His conscience, which was previously sleeping, begins to wake up. The arrow of conviction enters his consciousness, and the sinner, who before was free to go about his sinful pleasures, now begins to be afraid to go to his old haunts. God is now touching his conscience.

He did not care before. But when the Spirit of bondage comes upon the sinner it is the beginning of a change within his life. Samuel Rutherford says, 'God casts us down before conversion with the terrors of the law, making us see our miserable state, and that is the spirit of bondage.' The Puritan Robert Bolton says, 'The spirit of bondage must first be set on work to show us our spiritual misery, to humble us, to prepare for Christ.' The great Scottish theologian James Buchanan, in his book on the Holy Spirit, talks about the Philippian jailer of Acts 16 and says, 'From being a very careless man the Philippian jailer had now become a deeply convinced sinner, but not yet a converted man. These convictions were useful as preparatory means.'

I have taken time with this subject because this surely is what the Apostle Paul is referring to in Romans 8:15 where he speaks about 'the Spirit of bondage'. It is a theme which is neglected and overlooked today. The teaching is that when God is going to bring sinners to faith in Christ it is always his way to send the Holy Spirit upon them—perhaps not quite yet to convert them but, as it were, to hedge them in to a realization of their lost condition. It is a work which occurs in the soul and in the conscience just before sinners are brought to Christ.

Why does God do this? The answer is obvious. It is because sinners have no time for God, no wish for God, no desire for Christ, until they are driven to recognize their lost condition as men and women under bondage. We use two words in this connection: 'conviction' and 'compunction'. We do not often use the word 'compunction' any more, but it is a good word. What is the difference between conviction and compunction? An old writer says, 'In conviction, God lights a candle in the dark sinner's heart so that he may see the filth of his own life.' What, then, is compunction? In compunction the Holy Spirit takes the finger of the sinner and places it in the candle flame. He burns the finger and makes it feel pain. The sinner not only sees his sin, but feels the agony of being a sinner. That is what the Holy Spirit does in convicting us and giving us compunction. He shows the sinner the hatefulness of his sin and brings home to him his guilt, not simply in a notional way, mentally and intellectually, but in his conscience, until his conscience burns and smokes, and he feels his guiltiness before God.

The old preachers who knew that their great work was to bring sinners to Christ were not ashamed to preach the Moral Law to sinners before they preached the gospel to them. They believed that you can 'heal' people too soon. There is only one thing worse than being a sinner and that is to be a sinner who thinks he is saved when he is not. That is called in the Bible 'slight healing'. The old preachers, therefore, did not give sinners easy encouragement to believe they were converted. They sometimes left the sinner in the furnace of conviction a little while.

In this way the sinner is glad to get clear of sin and to come to the cross of Christ to find peace. That is what is referred to here by this expression 'the Spirit of bondage'. There is always an element of fear in a sinner's conversion if it is genuine: the fear is the realization that we are sinners in the hands of an angry God. However, God does not afflict us or wound us in order to kill us. He wounds us to heal us. He knocks us down to lift us up. He slays us so that we might have the resurrection of a new life.

This brings me, secondly, to speak about the new birth, or, as we also call it, regeneration. God may leave the sinner under these convictions for a greater or lesser time. John Bunyan tells us in his book *Grace Abounding* that he was kept by God in this state of conviction for a long time. God was pursuing him, as it were, so as to give him a deep sense of sin. But that state of fear does not continue in a Christian's experience for ever. God brings into the sinner's life this new birth, which is an act of God transforming the soul by implanting the seed of new life in the heart. The new birth is God's work and not man's. It is a birth from above. It is the life of God coming into the soul of man. It is not something in which the sinner cooperates. We do not choose Christ and then become Christians; we choose Christ only *after* we have been born of the Spirit of God.

It is most important that we should see that the new birth always comes before faith, and that we cannot believe until we have had the new birth; we cannot repent until we have had the new birth; we cannot begin to do anything right until we have had the new birth. The new birth is God's free gift, and we do not cooperate in it.

We do cooperate in sanctification and in justification. But we do not cooperate in the new birth. It is a sovereign act of God, and it is God's work alone. Of his will we are begotten to become the first-fruits of his creatures.

This is a lost emphasis in evangelistic preaching today. It is God's work to give grace to the soul. We are entirely dependent upon the mercy of God. We are thrown on the kindness of God. And this is what is done by the Spirit of bondage. He makes us see that we are nothing and that God is all in all. He brings us to see that our sins and iniquities are infinite, that we have no claims upon God as sinners, that we cannot compel God to do something for us. We cannot earn it, we cannot work for it, we cannot will it. We are thrown back, therefore, on this fact that we must plead with God for mercy, and we must go to him for help. The new birth is the implantation of divine life in the soil of the sinner's heart, and it is always placed at the subconscious level. Nobody knows the moment of his new birth. It is impossible to know the time when you are born again. The moment of the new birth is a mystery known only to God. It precedes faith. Once the life of God is begun in the sinner's heart it will grow and increase throughout life. It is the foretaste of eternal glory, because that new work cannot be destroyed. All the powers of hell cannot eradicate that new life which is begun in the sinner's soul. It is God's work, and he will bring it to completion. He will never allow any of the powers of darkness to destroy what he has once begun.

So it is literally true: 'Once a Christian, always a Christian.' 'He which hath begun a good work in you will perform it until the day of Jesus Christ' (Phil. 1:6). That, therefore, is what the new birth does. It brings us new life, and that life is in Christ. It happens in an instant of time, and it transforms the will, the affections and the conscience, making a man a new creation. 'If any man be in Christ, he is a new creature: old things are passed away' (2 Cor. 5:17). He cannot love the world as once he did.

The believer has new affections, new aspirations, new ambitions, new desires. He may at first go back once or twice to his old haunts after conversion, but when he gets to them he will find that his old love for sin has gone. He will say to himself, 'Did I used to come to this place? What a fool I was! Did I waste my time in this company? Is that what I lived for? What a madman I was! Did I used to come to drink pints of beer with these people who are cursing God? I must have been asleep! Now I see that this world is a madhouse.' And out he will go, and he will live for God.

This is what the new birth does: it gives a man eyes to see reality. He sees God upon his throne. The fear of God possesses his life. He is now impelled by the love of Christ to live with a new ambition and a new desire. It is the expulsive power of a new affection. His desire now is to live for God, for truth and for the cause of righteousness. Those old friends of his who see the change may well suspect that it is the work of God. They may say, 'Is that our old friend? What's happened to him?' The answer, of course, is, 'God is now in this man. He is altogether different from what he used to be.'

So, first of all, there is the work of the Spirit of God as a Spirit of preparation; and then there is the new birth. Thirdly, and finally, I must say a little concerning the Spirit of adoption.

Adoption means coming into God's family, becoming a child of God. It is the highest privilege of all. Justification is a great privilege, but adoption is a greater. Justification puts us right in the eyes of God's law, but adoption places us within God's very family. Professor John Murray says of adoption, 'It is the apex of privilege—the acme of privilege.' Dr J. I. Packer says, 'It is the highest privilege that the gospel offers.' You cannot put it any stronger than that.

However, there is a difference between adoption and the Spirit of adoption. Adoption is what we receive, but the Spirit of adoption is *assurance* of what we receive. That is not quite the same thing. If you read carefully the Westminster Confession and Catechisms and the good old books of the Puritans you will discover that they leave a place for people who may be Christians but who do not yet have assurance of that fact. There are such people. They are truly born again and show every evidence of it, but they have very little assurance of God's love for *them*.

How, then, do we get this Spirit of adoption? This Spirit of adoption is that full assurance of faith, the Holy Spirit witnessing with our spirits that we are the sons of God: 'The Spirit itself beareth witness with our spirit, that we are the children of God' (Rom. 8:16). So, clearly, this Spirit of adoption refers to the assurance, the certainty, the conviction, that we are God's children.

There are two ways in which we must come, and do come, to assurance. One way is to read the promises of God to believers and take them to heart. God says to us that if we love our brothers and sisters in Christ, it proves that we are Christians. 'We know that we have passed from death unto life, because we love the brethren' (1 John 3:14). If I love Christians because they are Christians, it proves I am a Christian. Again, if I love the Bible and if I love holiness, it is a sign and an evidence that I am born again. Nobody can love these things who is not born again. We refer to that way of arguing as the 'practical syllogism'. A syllogism is a way of reasoning. So the practical syllogism is this: God says that those who love Christians are Christians. And I love Christians. Therefore, I must be a Christian. That is a legitimate way of reasoning. We look for evidences and marks of grace, things that show that we belong to God.

But that is not the full-orbed assurance which it is possible for Christians to have. It is what we call a 'lower level' of assurance. It is all right as far as it goes, but there is much more assurance than that to be had. How much more?

When the Holy Spirit comes upon the Christian as a Spirit of adoption and God pours the Spirit upon the sinner's heart, there is an effect in the consciousness of the Christian whereby he knows—he feels—the love of God. This is something more than that practical syllogism: this is the direct witness of the Holy Spirit upon our own spirits that we are God's children. We refer to this as 'heaven upon earth'. It may happen suddenly, or it may come about gradually, but it is a most sublime, heavenly, strengthening experience; and we must not rest in any form of assurance short of this direct witness of God's Spirit with our spirit that we are the children of God.

The Westminster Confession refers to this as 'infallible assurance'. What a phrase! It makes a man as strong in the faith as a lion. When a man has had this, he is ready to face the world.

How could a man like Luther face the whole world? Through this assurance. How could the apostles go all round the Mediterranean preaching the gospel in defiance of the powers of their day? They had this assurance. How did the early Methodists go all round England when people threw stones and dead cats at them as they stood in market squares, lifting up their hands in preaching? The answer is this confidence in God, this assurance that they belonged to God.

We live in an age when we need again to ask God for a greater measure of this assurance than ever we have had before. It is possible for us to have more and more of this certainty—more and more of this holy boldness. It is the gift of the Holy Spirit bearing witness with our spirits that we are the sons of God.

I am reminded of the well-known story of the two great English Reformers Latimer and Ridley. The year was 1555. The Queen at that time is known as 'Bloody Mary'. She put about four hundred Protestants to death in her terrible reign of persecution, and in 1555 Latimer and Ridley were put to death by being burnt at Oxford. The brushwood was all round their feet, the torches of flame were put to the wood, and the flames were soon licking up into their faces. What did Latimer say in this situation? 'Be of good comfort, Master Ridley, and play the man: we shall this day light such a candle by God's grace, in England, as I trust shall never be put out.' How did he have that boldness? He said, 'When I live in a settled and steadfast assurance about the state of my soul, methinks I am as bold as a lion!' That's what we need to be—bold as lions.

Take the words of American theologian Samuel Finlay of Princeton, New Jersey, as he was dying: 'A Christian's death is the best part of his experience.' Friends gathered at the bedside said to him, 'Would you rather live or die, sir?' His answer? 'I would rather die.'

Christians die well. Worldly persons may, if they so choose, laugh us to scorn. They can mock us if they please.

They can tell us that we are old fashioned. But they will never die as well. A Christian dies well because he knows that he is right with God.

That is how these wonderful words in Romans 8:15–16 show us the beginning of true sanctification and of that great assurance which is the inheritance of men and women who belong to Jesus Christ.

FOUR

Through Fire and Water

For thou, O God, hast proved us: thou hast tried us, as silver is tried. Thou broughtest us into the net; thou laidst affliction upon our loins. Thou hast caused men to ride over our heads; we went through fire and through water: but thou broughtest us out into a wealthy place.—Psa. 66:10–12.

One of the great mistakes made in our day by many evangelical Christians is to suppose that God is aiming at our happiness. That is a false attitude towards the Christian's life. God is not aiming at our present happiness, but at our future happiness. And there is only one way to happiness, and that is through holiness. God, who is wise, is therefore in this life aiming at the Christian's holiness, because holiness is the way to happiness in the end. That might seem an obvious statement to make, but it is a most important way in which to look at the Christian life.

The vision which the biblical writers have is that God does not aim primarily at our present happiness here in this world. If he did, we could never understand books like the book of Job. There was not a greater man in that age than

Job, even on the testimony of God himself. But having announced to us the eminence of his servant Job, God proceeds to subject him to tremendous pressure, temptation, privation, suffering and loss. Indeed, he is stripped naked of everything, and escapes only, as he puts it, by the skin of his teeth.

If God were aiming at the happiness of his people here in this world, he would never allow such treatment, loss or affliction to come upon them. It often troubles God's people why, if he loves them, he allows them to go through pain and loss. Some Christians who are not very well taught say things like this: 'It is not our heavenly Father's will that we should suffer illness or trouble.' Some would even go a little further and say that it is the will of God that in this life, as Christians, we should be always happy. That is, as I have said, to misunderstand the intention of God.

It is true that God is aiming at our happiness in the end. But even then we must say that our happiness is in subordination to the glory of God. God is first of all aiming at his own glory in everything, and then he aims at his people's good in everything. But that is not the same as saying that in this life he aims at his people's happiness. Certainly, he does not aim at that first of all. Consequently, in this life we must accustom ourselves to suffering, hardship, disappointment and troubles of many kinds.

Let me quote the great Samuel Rutherford (you could hardly do a better thing for your own soul than to read

Rutherford's letters): 'Sanctification is the stormy north side of Christ.' In other words, sanctification is the hard part of the Christian life. Sanctification is not, for example, like the climate here in Adelaide. It is like the climate of the north of Scotland—often windy, rainy, snowy, cold, stormy. Of course, we must not exaggerate that; there are many comforts even there. But God is aiming at our sanctification first, not at our happiness first.

The well-balanced Christian life has three elements to it: firstly, doctrine; secondly, duty; and thirdly, experience. The Christian life is, therefore, like a three-legged stool. A two-legged stool will not stand, but a three-legged stool will. What do we mean by these three elements? Doctrine, of course, is what we believe—the body, the substance, of our belief; the confession of that knowledge which God has revealed in his word. We call it doctrine or theology. That is primary. We must be sound in our belief. If we are not sound at that point, we shall be sound in no point. Doctrine is like the locomotive to the train: it leads all the carriages. If we are right in doctrine, the probability is that we shall be right—or largely right—in the rest. If wrong, then wrong in the rest. Doctrine comes first.

Then, secondly, there is the element of practice, which is the same as our duty. The duty of the Christian is to 'work out [his] own salvation with fear and trembling' (Phil. 2:12) in terms of the rule which God has given to guide the practice of our life. This is the Moral Law. The Christian is not under the law as a covenant, but he is to obey the law as his rule. We are divorced from the Moral Law as the source of our life. Christ is the source of our life. But the Moral Law is given to us in order to show us the pattern for our life. Putting it another way, we say that the Moral Law is a schoolmaster to bring us to Christ that we might be justified; but as soon as we are justified in and by Christ, Christ takes us back to the Moral Law as the rule of our duty. So if we ask the question 'How can I please my Lord?' we are not left to guesswork or speculation; we are not just to go by feelings, impressions or suggestions of men. We are to go by his written word. Jesus says, 'If ye love me, keep my commandments' (John 14:15).

Then, thirdly, in addition to doctrine and practice there is this element of experience. This is different from the other two. The doctrine we believe is the same for us all, and the duty which we have towards God and man is the same for us all. There is one body of doctrine, one theology, one set of rules, for the whole church. There are not two theologies; there are not two types of Moral Law. These things are common to all believers in all ages. But experience is different. Each Christian's experience differs from that of every other Christian. You could say that God tailors a life for each one of his children. Imagine a mother with six children—six boys, let us say. In some cases, as they get older and too big for their clothes, they can hand them down to the others. But if there is a very tall fellow, they can't pass anything down to him because he is too big—he cannot wear his brother's clothes. In a similar way, God tailors a special life with its own distinctive experiences for every one of his children, and you cannot pass on your experience to anybody else. What you have experienced yourself will help others, but they cannot enter entirely into your experience. So while doctrine and practice are common to us all, experience is personal. We refer to this as God's providential will for our lives.

There is an ethical will which is the same for us all: that is the Moral Law. But his providential will is different. For example, take the patriarchs Abraham, Isaac, Jacob and Joseph. They were all good and godly men who walked with the Lord. They were all saved men. They all believed the same doctrine. They all had the same Moral Law. But each one had a very distinct experience which was the gift of God to him in particular. Abraham's life was an intensely active life. Isaac's life, by contrast, was a more passive life; it can be told more or less in one chapter. But when we come to Jacob, he had an intensely active life, and his experiences cover many chapters of Scripture because they are so varied and full. When you come to Joseph, you see he had an extraordinary providence. God had ordained for him experiences which were almost unique. He was sold by his own brothers into slavery in Egypt. There he became Prime Minister, administering the resources of the nation, influencing the whole civilized world—saving the world, you could say.

What an extraordinary life! God ordained these distinctive experiences for each of these patriarchs, and they were different in every case. No two are the same.

So it is with the people I am addressing here today or with any other audience of God's people. You all have the same faith; you all have the same practice. But, when it comes to experience, no two of you are the same. Some of you come here relatively carefree; others are burdened and troubled; and so on. You should, therefore, be very kind to the person sitting next to you because you may not know the burdens they carry, and you may be quite incapable of guessing the trials through which they are passing. You may not know what sleepless nights they have had tossing on their bed, wrestling in prayer, for reasons of their own health, for fears, for temptations, for trials, for sorrows, for the approach of death.

We know nothing about what is going on in our neighbour's mind because the experiences of each one are what we may call the real-life situation in which that man or woman lives. Here in God's house and in the conferences we enjoy together we are in God's classroom. When we come to the services of the sanctuary we are learning the theory. But as soon as we go out there, back home and to work, college or school, there is the practice and outworking of it.

It is easy to take in the theory, but, as you know from experience, the hard thing is to work out the theory in a real-life situation. It is easy enough to sit in church and listen to some eloquent preacher opening up the word of God to you. He does the work and you sit down and take it in. But what you hear you then have to take with you into your real-life situation, and the theory has to be worked out in practice in the workplace, school or office. There is the difficulty—working out our salvation 'with fear and trembling. For it is God which worketh in [us] both to will and to do of his good pleasure' (Phil. 2:12–13). You could say that this is the drill room of the Christian soldier, but out there you are in the real world of conflict and the theatre of battle. Here is the drill floor; there is the real war.

All that I have said relates very closely to Psalm 66:10–12. The text tells us that God proves his people. It is, if you like, a historical psalm. The writer, whoever he was—David, Asaph or some other—is talking about how God dealt with his own people. And it is applicable to us individually. God proves his people; God tries us. The Scottish Examination Board's motto is 'Everything will be weighed in the balances'. You can see the fitness of that: an examination board needs to warn the scholars that everything they are supposed to be learning will be proved and tried when they sit down in the examination room. That will prove how much or how little they have learned. That is the experience which is referred to in Psalm 66:10. God will prove us. He will try us.

What we learn here in our churches will be tested in real-life situations. We do not just come to church or to conferences out of pure academic interest. There is that element, of course. But what we learn or profess to have learnt, God will place in the balance. God will have us put to the trial and to the test.

This writer in the psalm then uses several metaphors implying various kinds of test. First of all, he uses the illustration of smelting precious metal: 'Thou hast tried us, as silver is tried.' I don't know very much about smelting precious metals, but I suppose you take the silver ore and place it in some metal container, like a pan, and then you subject it to intense heat; and I presume that the ore melts and the scum—the worthless element—rises to the top, and the precious metal floats in a liquid form at the bottom of this pan. Then I suppose the skilful refiner comes along with something like a scraper and he skims off the scum on the top until he has the purified metal. Perhaps he has to do it several times.

In Psalm 12 the Bible is compared to precious silver refined seven times. This indicates that you refine it and refine it and refine it. The Bible is solid silver, solid gold, through and through. There is no error, no impurity, here: it is the solid, pure, real precious metal. God similarly refines the Christian. He refines us as silver is refined. We call this the process of sanctification: growing in grace and in holiness. It is the fruit of God's process of subjecting us to various forms of heat. I think you would agree that the metaphor is a very suitable one.

There are real-life situations in which we are subjected

to tremendous heat, as it were. God places us in situations in which we find ourselves in great difficulties. He did this with Job and with Abraham. Remember the test which God gave to Abraham in Genesis 22:2: 'Take now thy son, thine only son Isaac, whom thou lovest, and get thee into the land of Moriah; and offer him there for a burnt offering.' What questions must have arisen in Abraham's mind: 'My own son? But I have waited years for this son of promise!' And then the objection: 'But from this son the Messiah will come!' But in faith, Abraham closed his lips and went on his way. God was refining him as silver is refined. And God will do that with you and with me. Ministers normally have to go through more of this than other Christians, because the minister has to go through experiences to help his people, and God will subject the minister and the faithful elder to experiences which others may not know of, so that they may be a help to other people in the course of life.

The smelting of precious metal is the first of the psalmist's illustrations of the sanctifying processes of God's divine will for his people. The second illustration, in Psalm 66:11, is slightly different. The psalmist says, 'Thou broughtest us into the net.' This metaphor is that of a wild animal—a bull, boar or some other powerful beast—caught in a net which the hunter has arranged with camouflage. Perhaps he has covered the net with leaves, and then chased the animal, who in fear and alarm runs in the direction of the net, only to discover that he is caught in its snare. The more the animal thrashes about with its hoofs, the worse its situation becomes, until in exhaustion it can only lie on the ground and is an easy prey for the hunter. God may do that to us.

Sometimes the Christian is like a bull in a net. He thrashes about to get clear of his duties or troubles. That experience of being caught in a net was part of God's dealings with you to sanctify you—to make you a better child of God.

As an illustration, let me tell a story to my own disadvantage. It is amazing what experiences we have to go through in the course of preparing to address audiences. Years ago, I was invited to address a conference in Britain, and *everything* went wrong, from start to finish. First of all, I lost my way to the venue and was late. Everybody was waiting, and I had the humbling experience of coming half an hour late into the pulpit. Believe me, it is not an experience to be coveted! Then the pulpit was so low that I could not see my notes; and the light above was so dim I could not read them; and my throat was so poor with a throat infection that I could not articulate my words! You can guess that when I had finished this gruelling experience I was looking for a deep hole to drop into. I was tempted to say, as I went away, 'Never again. *Never* again.' What an experience!

But God sometimes teaches us more through our failures than through our supposed successes. And those things that we most dread, both in anticipation and in experience, are the things whereby God may do us most good.

Then the psalmist changes the metaphor again in Psalm

66:12: 'Thou hast caused men to ride over our heads.' This is an extraordinary experience. God takes his children and he lays them out on the motorway, and he keeps them pinned down there on the road, as it were, while men ride over them in their cars, buses and lorries—to use the illustration of this text. What does this illustration mean? It means that God sometimes puts his children into such a position that men treat them like dirt. Men trample all over us with their words and their attitudes. People can be very cruel and unkind to us as believers.

There are many illustrations of this in Scripture. Joseph was sold by his brothers into Egypt. The prophets were treated like dirt. Isaiah, according to tradition, was sawn in half. Jeremiah was thrown into the dungeon, then carried off to Egypt by his fellow countrymen. Daniel was put in the lions' den. The first Christian martyr, Stephen, was stoned to death.

Supremely, of course, the Saviour of the world, Jesus Christ, was treated terribly. As soon as he was born, soldiers came from Herod to kill him. He had to be rescued. As soon as he had preached his first sermon in the synagogue in Nazareth, his own home town, they marched him to the brow of the hill to throw him over. Had it not been for his supernatural power to walk through the midst of them and go on his way, he would have been killed before he had really begun his ministry. And everybody knows how our Lord suffered at last on the cross.

We must expect that. It is part of our sanctification that God would subject us from time to time to the cruel dealings of men. I doubt very much if there is any Christian who has not experienced it. But let us learn this much: to be kind to one another; to speak kindly to one another and of one another. We have problems enough from the world without saying ungracious things to and about one another as believers.

But then the psalmist changes the metaphor again in Psalm 66:12: 'We went through fire and through water.' This is the most dreadful experience of all. Fire and water are terrible elements for man. In water we drown; in fire we burn. Neither experience is one we would wish to have. I remember once talking to a woman who nearly drowned. She told me her experience. She said she went down, and then she came up again, and went down for the second time and up again. Nobody was there to rescue her. She expected to die. Her mind was full of thoughts and memories. Mercifully, somebody did rescue her in the nick of time. What an experience!

Or take the case of those who have been rescued from fire. John Wesley, who became leader of the Methodist movement and one of the great Methodists, had to be rescued from fire as a child in the rectory at Epworth. Dr Lloyd-Jones too, I believe, was rescued as a child from fire—like a brand, plucked from the burning. It is not an enviable experience, but God does that.

But notice what is said at the end of Psalm 66:12: 'but'. There is always this divine 'but' in Scripture. Having done all these things, the psalmist says, 'Thou broughtest us out into a wealthy place.' All the Christian's trials are ordained for his good. All things are working together for his good. It does not look like it; it does not seem like it; it does not feel like it. But it is so.

Hannah put it perfectly in her famous song in the first book of Samuel: 'The LORD killeth, and maketh alive: he bringeth down to the grave, and bringeth up' (1 Sam. 2:6)—he casts us down, and lifts us up again. That is why God deals with us in this way: it is to bring us to a place that is wealthy. What is that wealthy place? It is holiness of character. Through these trails and tribulations God is improving our character. We are the better for being refined; for being in the net; for having men ride over us; for going through fire and water. How? It is because in this way God shakes us free of the dirt of our sins.

You know what happens to, let us say, a little dog. Dogs are always very inquisitive. Little puppies go into all kinds of dirty places and their coats get covered in soot or soil. Then you wash the dog, and it is clean again. So it is with us. We need to be washed and shaken. When our clothes become dusty, we take them off, shake them and brush them. So God deals with his own children: he, as it were, shakes the dirt off us. And all these trials are in order that we might be pure and that we might be partakers of a holy nature and a holy character. He sweetens us, he makes us more spiritual, more sympathetic, more kind, more understanding, more gracious, by these trails and tribulations.

Four experiences are very frequent in the lives of God's people. The first one I will refer to as divine humblings. None of us enjoys being humbled. It does not matter how humble you are; you do not enjoy being humbled. Bunyan, in his great book *The Pilgrim's Progress*, refers to the 'Valley of Humiliation' which the pilgrim had to go through. God ordains that experience from time to time. You will discover that God will take you by a circuitous route in life in which you are deeply mortified and humbled by the ways in which he deals with you. You were made to be seen in your worst colours. You were made to appear in the worst light. You were uncomfortable because everything went a little bit wrong. We were almost exposed in our nakedness. We made mistakes. People saw through us, and they thought the worst of us. All of that is very mortifying, very humbling to flesh and blood.

What is the wealthy place to which this brings us? I believe that through the Valley of Humiliation God would bring us to the place where we see that it does not matter what people think of us. If we ever once learn that lesson we are wealthy indeed. It is a terrible bondage to be forever worried about what people think of us. And yet we are all inclined to that infirmity. We are so sensitive to what people think. 'What does he think of me? What are they saying about me?' But you know the old saying: 'They say. Who say? Let them say.' Does it matter what people think of us? Why are we not more concerned about what the Lord thinks of us? It is because of our sin. We are too preoccupied with what men say about us. But God will shake this wickedness out of us, and the way he does it is by taking us often through the Valley of Humiliation until we lose our good looks and we cease to care whether people love us or not. Provided only that we can be pleasing to God, we care little about what men may say. You know, that is the making of a minister. A minister is one who not only has to say the truth, but he has to say it whether men love him or loathe him for what he says. He must be faithful to the word of God though everyone should sneer at him for what he says.

The second of these divine experiences which God will give us is that from time to time, if we are not very vigilant, we shall discover that God will allow us to do things which are not for our good. A young woman, let us say, feels that her years are passing by and she has no husband. And then along comes a young man who is not a Christian. He starts to attend church and pays attention to her. She says to herself, 'Well, maybe if I marry this unconverted man I can convert him to faith in Christ.' And then, perhaps, in a moment of weakness she says, 'I know the Bible forbids this, but perhaps it will work out.' She may then get married to him, to her eventual sorrow.

That is only one example of very many. From time to

time God may allow us to do things which are very hurtful to ourselves. We know what is right. We know his word, his will—but we do not always do it. There are many applications of it. The psalmist says, 'He gave them their request; but sent leanness into their soul' (Psa. 106:15). May God keep us from making that kind of mistake! We have all made mistakes along the pilgrimage. But let us pray God never to give us over to do what we ought not to do.

The third experience which I might mention is that of divine chastenings. When we were children our parents chastised us. God chastens us for our good like a faithful parent. When you and I commit foolish mistakes and sin against him, we are treated as children and not as bastards. God will chastise us. We all have recollections of that, don't we? But the wealthy place is this: we become sweeter for it.

You see what a child is like when he has been cheeky and unkind to his mother. Along comes his father and says, 'You will take that back and apologize to Mother.' 'I shan't,' says the child. 'Won't you? Right. Come here.' And old-fashioned justice is administered until tears change the child's mind and he rushes to his mother's skirt and says, 'I'm sorry, Mother. I didn't mean it. I'm sorry.'

You see, we are sweeter for chastisement. We need it. We are at times too bold; we think we know best. And so the Lord lays his hand upon us and we smart for it. Let us be thankful for divine chastisement. It brings us to a wealthy place, in that we become partakers of God's holiness.

Then, fourthly, there is another painful experience: God can plough up our corruptions to show us what is in our own hearts.

In Scotland, as probably all over the world, we have tractors that plough up the fields before sowing time. The tractor driver goes up and down the field with his plough, making long, straight furrows. As he does so, you see a lot of birds following the plough. Why? Because the birds see that the ground is full of worms, and they descend on those worms.

That is what God does to our hearts. Our hearts are nothing but a can of worms. Christ said about us, 'For from within, out of the heart of men, proceed evil thoughts, adulteries, fornications, murders, thefts, covetousness, wickedness, deceit, lasciviousness, an evil eye, blasphemy, pride, foolishness' (Mark 7:21–22). Christ did not say that to malign us, but because it is the plain truth.

Every evil thing is in my nature, and in yours, and in every child of Adam's. The Apostle Paul says, 'When I would do good, evil is present with me … O wretched man that I am! who shall deliver me from the body of this death?' (Rom. 7:21, 24). From time to time, therefore, God will plough up our hearts and he will show us the can of worms that resides within us—not a nice sight. Oh, what pride is in our nature! What self-love! What arrogance! What disobedience! Have you discovered that? There are some Christians who do not know themselves. But by ploughing up our hearts, God brings us to the wealthy place. What is that? It is that we learn to know ourselves.

John Calvin begins his excellent book *The Institutes of the Christian Religion* with this emphasis: We need to know God, and we need to know ourselves. That is where all knowledge begins: to know God, and to know oneself. And we do not know ourselves until we know God; and when we know God he will teach us about ourselves and show us what is in our hearts. He will perform 'open-heart surgery' many a time and show us the depravity within ourselves. 'The heart is deceitful above all things, and desperately wicked: who can know it?' (Jer. 17:9).

The purpose of God in this experience of bringing us through fire and water is that we might become more holy. At last, in heaven, we shall be blessed with eternal happiness. In this life God is changing us so that the tin becomes iron, and the iron becomes brass, and then the brass, silver. At last, the silver will become gold.

FIVE

Left in the World

I pray not that thou shouldest take them out of the world, but that thou shouldest keep them from the evil.—John 17:15.

We have already had occasion to say that there is a close connection between sanctification and glorification, in this respect: that sanctification is glory begun here in this life, while glorification will be the completion of sanctification in the life to come. They are related as the bud is related to the flower, and so we should strive after sanctification, or holiness of life, with all our hearts here in this present world.

These two themes come into the prayer of our Saviour in John 17. At verse 17 he says to his heavenly Father, 'Sanctify them [that is, his own people] through thy truth: thy word is truth.' So one of the great means, indeed the *principal* means, whereby God sanctifies his people in this life is through the word of truth. That is not simply the word read, but the word preached. Preaching, therefore, is essential to our sanctification.

But also at the end of the prayer our Lord looks beyond sanctification to glorification. We see this in verse 24: 'Father, I will that they also, whom thou hast given me, be with me where I am; that they may behold my glory, which thou hast given me: for thou lovedst me before the foundation of the world.'

We refer to this prayer of Christ as the great High Priestly prayer. Jesus is not praying in a private capacity here. We often pray as private individuals, and so we must; but Christ here is praying as the great Head of the church. He is the representative of all those who are or will be his; and they constitute one collective whole. Our Lord is concerned about this fact of oneness because in the course of his prayer he prays that they 'all may be one as we are'. In the mind of Christ were those believers who were living at that time as well as those believers who would be living in after-time. The many believers who were not then living were in his mind, his purpose, his decree. At that time you and I were in the womb of God's eternal purpose. But we were certain to be born because the decree of God renders all things certain. And we were certain to be converted—if we are Christians—because the decree of God guarantees that all those for whom Christ died will come to faith.

Notice that our Lord does not pray for all the world. He actually uses a very distinct phrase. He says, 'I pray not for the world, but for them which thou hast given me; for they are thine. And all mine are thine, and thine are mine' (verses 9–10). So it is very clear that Christ had in mind a distinct group of persons living and to live in the future who were one body, one church. They were one united collective entity. They are referred to elsewhere in the Bible as the 'elect' of God. These are they whom God loved from eternity, for whom Christ prays and for whom he died. They will come to the knowledge of the truth. And they will and must be saved.

The High Priestly office of Christ involved him in three particular works. The work of a priest was three-fold: it was to teach, to pray and to offer sacrifice. If you study the Old Testament you will notice that these three elements entered into the priest's work, and, of course, they enter into Christ's work. He teaches, he prays and he offers sacrifice.

His teaching was now virtually complete. For three years before this prayer, our Lord had been teaching his disciples and, indeed, many others who came to listen to his sermons. Here he teaches the disciples exclusively. In John 14, 15 and 16—those sublime chapters which are referred to sometimes as the 'inner sanctuary'—we learn not a few of the things which he taught his disciples.

But here in chapter 17 he turns from teaching and preaching to praying, and this wonderful chapter consists of our Lord's High Priestly prayer in which, as I have already said, he prays for the entire collective church for whom he was to die. A few hours following this prayer, having finished his teaching and completed his praying, our Saviour was to offer his sacrifice—not of bulls or goats, but his very self. Our Lord loved the church and gave himself for it.

Perhaps you feel that you are not much of a Christian and you do not really count. You feel a mere nothing, a mere nobody. But if you are a Christian, you are one of those for whom the eternal Son of God came into this world and died. This shows you the love that God bears to you personally. We may often feel ourselves to be nothing, but if we are those for whom he died, we have reason to lift up our hearts in worship and thankfulness for the sovereign love and grace of God that made us to differ from others. Certainly we were not born different from others; we lived as 'children of wrath' in this world as all others do. By nature we are haters of God and haters of one another. So if today we love the truth it is by grace alone and by the goodness of Jesus Christ.

Let me just mention that while our Lord's prayer was prayed on earth, this intercessory work of Christ continues still in heaven. We are not to conceive of Christ interceding on his knees in heaven; it is not as though our Lord needs to put his hands together or close his eyes and go on his knees as we do. His very presence before the throne of God the Father in our human nature is itself an ongoing prayer. His proximity to the Father's throne constitutes in itself a prayer for all his church because he is the firstborn from the dead and the 'first-fruits'. His presence before God guarantees that all believing souls from Adam's day to the end of the world must appear in heaven at last. They are his eternally.

In the Old Testament the first-fruits were the first ripe grain which the farmer was told by God to cut and to wave before God as the pledge of the entire harvest to come. So Christ is the first-fruits—the firstborn from the dead. He appears before God as our representative, guaranteeing that we who love him and believe in him will come to glory and to heaven. That is what Christ is doing now. His very presence on high is for your sake and mine. He is there in your name and in mine, and he will not leave heaven until that appointed hour when the trumpet is blown by the angel and the dead are raised.

He will then appear in the clouds of heaven with glory, honour and power, encircled by all his worshipping angels and saints already dead in Christ, and then the graves will be opened and the dead bodies of all saints from all ages will rise again. They will appear like a cloud in the air to meet the Lord and to greet him. He will come to separate between his own and the wicked, and to say to his own people, 'Come, ye blessed of my Father, inherit the kingdom prepared for you from the foundation of the world.' And then to the wicked he will say, 'Depart from me, ye cursed, into everlasting fire, prepared for the devil and his angels' (Matt. 25:34, 41).

That will be the ultimate separation. The whole universe waits for that moment and that day. And the reason why the day of judgment does not come is because there are still those for whom Christ died in the world who are not yet born. They are in all nations. They must come—our brothers and sisters whom Christ loved as he loved us—and the end of the world will not come till they are brought in.

Now, verse 15 of my text states, 'I pray not that thou shouldest take them out of the world, but that thou shouldest keep them from the evil.' We will look at this under three divisions. Firstly, I will say what our Lord does *not* pray for. Secondly, I will give you reasons why our Lord prays in that negative way. And then, thirdly, I will say what he does positively pray: 'that thou shouldest keep them from the evil'.

So, firstly, what is it that our Lord does not pray for? 'I pray not that thou shouldest take them out of the world.' This is a surprising prayer because Christ is praying to his Father that God would not take us, his people, out of this world.

The world is a dangerous place, full of temptation, sin and evil. You and I would not desire this for our children. We do not put our children into dangerous situations if we can avoid it. We do not put our children to live in slums. I do not intend to speak unkindly or to be disrespectful of those who are poor or have to live in very poor homes. But we would not choose to put our children into an unpleasant area to live. Nor would we put them into schools where they would learn bad habits or be assailed by dangerous temptations, such as drugs and crime.

But God's wisdom is greater than ours, and it is the pleasure of God to leave his children in this 'slum' of a world, this dangerous world, for a time. That is a most interesting thing in itself, and we can only begin to understand the wisdom of God in that regard when we bear in mind what Christ has to say at the *end* of his prayer. There we see he has three great desires for his people. One of them is their unity: 'that they all may be one; as thou, Father, art in me, and I in thee, that they also may be one in us: that the world may believe that thou hast sent me' (verse 21). So our Lord is keeping his people in this world for a time intentionally to this end, that at the end of their journey, when their sanctification is complete, they will be one church, one body, one bride of Christ. That is why Jesus does not mind our being in this world for a time.

This world is not our rest; it is not our home; it is an alien place. Yet it is God's intention to keep us here for a while. So Jesus prays to his Father not to take us out of this world.

But then, secondly, our Lord prays at the end of this prayer not only that we might be one, but also that we might share his glory. He prays to his Father that we might behold his glory 'which thou gavest me' (verse 22).

This glory is the glory given to Christ as the God-man. In his divine nature Christ had and ever will have unchanging glory. He never lost his glory, but when he took human nature into union with himself at Bethlehem and became a child his glory was veiled over. His humanity appeared the same as our humanity. To have seen the face of Jesus in this life would not have impressed you with the sense that he was different from any other person. You would have thought him a typical Jew—a typical, ordinary man, the same as us. There was no special evidence on his face or body that he was different from others.

But he was the sinless Son of God, and when he had completed his work of living and dying for us he was raised by the glory of God. At his ascension he passed through degrees of exaltation until that same body of Jesus—that human body—now shines like the sun. When John in Revelation 1 saw a vision of Christ, he fell at his feet as dead. This is astonishing because John was close to Christ, so intimate, in fact, that John laid his head on Jesus' breast at the supper. But when he sees the vision of the glorified, exalted Christ, he falls at his feet as dead. And that indicates the measure in which our Saviour has been glorified by God as a reward for his completed work.

Our Lord prays that we may see that glory. This will be part of the destiny of the entire church of God. They will gaze upon the effulgence, the splendour, the radiance, of the face of Jesus Christ. We glimpse something of it now by faith in the Scriptures, but then we shall see for ourselves eternally the glory of our Redeemer.

Then, thirdly, our Lord also prays that we might be filled with his love. He prays that 'the love wherewith thou [the Father] hast loved me may be in them, and I in them' (verse

26). These three things explain why it is that Christ intends us, as Christians, to be in this world for a time.

There are many good reasons why we need to be in this world for a time, but I must observe that we *need* the afflictions of this life. They are good for us, because the afflictions of this life are sanctified afflictions. 'Tribulation', says Paul, 'worketh patience; and patience, experience; and experience, hope: and hope maketh not ashamed; because the love of God is shed abroad in our hearts by the Holy Ghost which is given unto us' (Rom. 5:3–5). Our tribulations are necessary. Every Christian would have to confess that there are many things in his life which give him difficulty and trial, sorrow and pain. But these very things, hard as they are, are being blessed to us in ways we do not know.

Samuel Rutherford said, 'Our pride needs winter weather to rot it.' Just as in a farm you have to rot down the vegetation in the winter so that it becomes good manure for the ground for the next season, so our pride—our arrogance—needs winter weather to rot it. We need, in other words, the frosts, that cold blast of the east wind. Cold weather rots down the vegetation. That is good for the ground. It kills the bacteria which are harmful to the next year's crop. So in our lives, we need the winter weather to rot and break down the arrogance within us.

It is only through much tribulation, then, that we are to expect to get to heaven. There is no getting to heaven without some tasting of tribulation in this world. The word 'tribulation' comes from the Latin word *tribulum*, a tool which consisted of two pieces of wood hinged together. Holding one piece of wood like a baton in one hand, and using the other as a flail, the farmer used the *tribulum* to separate the chaff from the grain at the time of harvest. That is how God sanctifies his people. Tribulation is the flagellum, the instrument in his hand, whereby he beats out the good corn and removes the chaff out of our lives.

So our Lord prays here that God would not take us out of the world, but that he would keep us from the evil. Let us remember this when trial and tribulation comes; when disappointment overshadows our lives; when bereavement crosses our path, when we have to say farewell to our loved ones and know the pain of loneliness; when God disappoints our expectations; and when life has its strange windings and turnings.

We may not understand why God should do this to us, or why we should have to go through such experiences. But let us never believe the lie of the devil, that trouble and sorrow are necessarily God's judgment upon us. That was the mistake made by Job's friends. Their philosophy was this foolish one: that God sends happiness in this life to those whom he loves, and pain in this life to those who do not honour him. That is true only in a limited measure. Very often in this life it is those whom God loves whom he chastises and afflicts with trouble, sorrow and pain. The reason is obvious: it is that we might become more Christ-like in our lives.

Secondly, let me give you some reasons why God has arranged things in this way. Why is it his good pleasure that we should not be taken to heaven at once? The first thing to say is this: it was quite possible for God, had he seen fit to do so, to have taken all his children out of this world. God, when he gives us the new birth, makes a wonderful change within our hearts. It is nothing short of a 'new creation'. The light that shines in the heart is as miraculous and supernatural as when God created the heavens and the earth in Genesis 1. The conversion of one soul is just as much an act of divine power and omnipotence as the creation of a new universe.

This raises the question, why did God not convert us in one instant and take us to heaven in the next? Surely that would have been a much more comfortable thing for me. God might have seen fit to do that. So why has the Almighty seen fit not to do that, but left us here in this world?

I would suggest, firstly, that God has acted in this way so that we might discover by experience what a wonderful change he has brought into our lives through the new birth. We are a wonder to ourselves. We can certainly say, 'I am not what I should be, I am not what I would be, but I am not what I *was*.' The Christian is amazed to discover how much of a change has occurred in his heart. We remember the days when we were unconverted. We remember that our love then was for the world and the things of the world. Like others who are not yet Christians, we were running in the ways of this world. We chased vain pleasure; we sought the things that gratify the flesh and the mind. We had little or no thought of God.

But now that we are converted, God is more than all else to us. God is the pole star of our life. God is the sun that shines every day in our hearts here below. God is more to us than life itself. 'For to me to live is Christ,' says the Christian, 'and to die is gain' (Phil. 1:21). So God has left us here for a few short years that we might realize how great a change conversion has brought into our lives.

Secondly, God has kept us in this world so that we might through long experience realize how sinful we are and how unworthy we are of the love of Christ! When we are first converted we do not really know ourselves. Yes, we use evangelical language because we realize the Bible tells us that we are sinners, and we say about ourselves at our first conversion, 'I am a sinner, and Christ died for sinners like me.' But we do not know what we are talking about. It takes a whole lifetime to discover just how sinful we are. It takes a long, long trial of our own wicked hearts to discover just what winding corridors of deception lurk in our nature; what dark shadows of wickedness, what hellish lusts, there are; what acts of unkindness we are capable of; what unkind things we are capable of saying; what dark suspicions we are capable of having.

We do not know these things except by years of experience of ourselves. That is what Paul refers to in Romans 7: from verse 14 onwards he refers to the Christian's self-knowledge. He discovers about himself that the good that he would do, he does not do; the evil he would not do is what he does do. It is not that he does not wish to do the will of God, but his sad experience is that he *cannot* do all the good that he wishes to do. There is a law within the Christian called the law of sin and death. It is there working in him still, and it brings him into bondage, in a measure. It is impossible for us to be perfect.

Thirdly, God has left us in this world in order that we may groan for heaven and yearn to be delivered from the body of this death. That is why the Apostle Paul says in 2 Corinthians 5:2, 'For in this [our earthly house] we groan, earnestly desiring to be clothed upon with our house which is from heaven.' It is 'not for that we would be unclothed', he says, 'but clothed upon, that mortality might be swallowed up of life' (verse 4). It is not that we are ambitious to die and become 'unclothed' so much as that we are ambitious for the resurrection. Our great hope as Christians is not the grave; it is the resurrection from the grave. The Christian is content to die and to become 'unclothed', if necessary. By this metaphor of being unclothed Paul means that we lose our body for a time, and the body is laid in the wardrobe of the earth until the trumpet sounds. Then that suit of clothes laid in the grave is quickened again by the power of God and raised from the grave. So we put on our new suit of clothes. It is the old body that we now have, but wonderfully renewed—

rejuvenated, beautified, glorified. In the resurrection day we wear that suit of clothes for ever. These are things which we know here in this life, and because we know this we groan, longing for that day.

This body which is now a trial to us will soon be brighter than the sun itself, radiant with the reflected glory of our blessed Redeemer. So in this life we groan, and we need to have the experience of groaning. That is the intention of God. And so Christ said, 'I pray not that thou shouldest take them out of the world.'

Now, thirdly, what *does* Christ pray for his people here? We have seen, firstly, the negative side of this text from verse 15, 'I pray not that thou shouldest take them out of the world.' Secondly, I have given you a few reasons why God in his wisdom has seen fit to keep us in this world. But now, thirdly and lastly, what is it positively that Christ does pray for his people here? 'I pray', he says, 'that thou shouldest keep them from the evil' (verse 15). One of the evils in mind must be that of being deceived by the devil and of returning to a condition of sin. The devil would dearly love to snatch us all from the power of God and bring us back into bondage to a love of the world. Sometimes he succeeds for a time, but he never succeeds altogether. So our experience of the devil's wicked power should teach us to watch and pray. We are saints living in a sinful world. We are pilgrims and strangers. We have no business dallying with sin. We must keep ourselves unspotted from the world as far as we can. We must plough a straight furrow between here and heaven. We are to walk the narrow path as carefully as we can. Make sure that you get to heaven cleanly, that you have no falls. Bring no shame on yourself and no dishonour on your Lord. Bring a clean testimony with you, and a clean bill of health as one who has shunned evil.

That is what our Lord prays for: that we may get safe home to heaven; that God would keep us from the evil. This word 'evil' could mean 'the evil one', the devil, or it may be sin. Either way it amounts much to the same thing.

We are not on our own as believers in this life. Round about us, going before us, underneath us, are the everlasting arms. God is with us on the way. We are being kept by the power of God through faith unto salvation. Make sure you get safely to the heavenly feast and so sit down with Abraham, Isaac and Jacob in the kingdom of God. You are being called to the wedding supper of the Lamb.

You are being preserved safe unto life eternal. That is what our Lord intends by his prayer here. And it is surely a tremendous reassurance to us. We are not on our own. In the life situations in which we find ourselves, God promises always to be with us. His grace is sufficient for us in all the contingencies of life. Whatever you are to face, God will give you grace enough to face it. And that is a great strength.

There is another evil: it is the evil of false doctrine. If the devil cannot catch us with temptations of a worldly kind, he will attack us by temptations of a religious kind. If we are church-goers the devil will try to catch us out by false teaching. So we need to watch very carefully as we travel from here to heaven so that we are not snared by false doctrine. Too many are. There are all manner of false teachings in this world which allure and seduce men from the path.

Even within the evangelical church there are many strange doctrines floating about which damage men's souls. And so our wisdom is to look carefully to our going. We must look carefully to make sure that, whatever we are taught in our churches and in our fellowships, we believe nothing but the word of God. Check to see that everything you read and hear is the word of God. Do not take it on credit. Do not go after experience for experience's sake. Make sure that it is not simply your emotions that lead you along, but that your mind is well informed with the teaching of Holy Scripture. This, of course, is the reason for reading the best books and studying the best theology. It is so that you may understand the dangers of false teaching and be the more on your guard against them. But, thank God, we are not left on our own, even in connection with false teaching. Christ has prayed for all his people that they would be preserved from false doctrine. We must be watchful, therefore, and cooperate with his grace and with his intercession in heaven, and not receive anything which is not according to the word of God.

But let me conclude with this: when Christ prays here that we might be kept from the evil, I believe this includes despair. Despair is a very real evil. God's people in this life sometimes have such sorrow and such disappointment that they are almost swallowed up with grief.

How does God keep us from the evil of despair? It is by meeting us many times along our pilgrim way with the fresh oil of gladness. God knows how to anoint our heads with fresh oil. He knows how to put the cup of cheer and comfort to our lips. He knows how much tribulation we can take and how much we cannot. And God in his goodness will cause us to be anointed afresh with comfort and encouragement. He will spread a table before us even in the presence of our enemies. Our cup will run over. Goodness and mercy will follow us all the days of our life, so that we may dwell at last in the house of the Lord for ever.

We must believe that God's purposes are invincible. Nothing in heaven or earth or under the earth can ever interrupt the sovereign purposes of God. Christ has come. Christ has died. Christ intercedes. Christ is coming. And all those for whom he died will come. They shall come from the north, the south, the east and the west, they will enter the kingdom of God, and there they will take their place. No matter how dark the situation may seem to be today, we must believe that God's work is going on steadily in his preordained power and grace. We must believe that God is calling men and women to himself. For your encouragement I would say that there are probably more Christians living in the world today than ever there were living in any previous generation.

God's word is being fulfilled. There are many churches and many shining Christians in the nations. Go to Korea, for instance, and you will see this. Look at America: truly it is an amazing land with many true gospel churches. The word of God is calling Christ's people home to God. It is happening all over the world, and it will go on happening till all those for whom Christ prays are saved.

So let us press on, knowing that when we get safe home to heaven he will say to everyone who has been faithful to him in this world: 'Well done, good and faithful servant; thou hast been faithful over a few things, I will make thee ruler over many things: enter thou into the joy of thy lord' (Matt. 25:23). And when you hear that, you will be comforted eternally for the few tribulations that you were called to undergo in this short life.

SIX

Union and Communion with Christ

I am the true vine, and my Father is the husbandman. Every branch in me that beareth not fruit he taketh away: and every branch that beareth fruit, he purgeth it, that it may bring forth more fruit. Now ye are clean through the word which I have spoken unto you. Abide in me, and I in you. As the branch cannot bear fruit of itself, except it abide in the vine; no more can ye, except ye abide in me. I am the vine, ye are the branches: He that abideth in me, and I in him, the same bringeth forth much fruit: for without me ye can do nothing. If a man abide not in me, he is cast forth as a branch, and is withered; and men gather them, and cast them into the fire, and they are burned. If ye abide in me, and my words abide in you, ye shall ask what ye will, and it shall be done unto you. Herein is my Father glorified, that ye bear much fruit; so shall ye be my disciples.—John 15:1–8.

The subject of these addresses, you will recall, is that of sanctification and glorification. That is to say, it is the work of God whereby he sanctifies our lives as Christians here in this world, and prepares us for glory in the world which is to come. As I have said, these two things are connected. There is no way that a man or woman is going to be glorified in heaven unless he or she is sanctified in this life.

Sanctification begins with the new birth. Before we are born again by the Spirit of God we cannot even begin to be holy. No unconverted man has ever begun to be holy. There is no sanctification until we come to Christ. But when we are in Christ and are born again, a process begins to take place which we refer to as sanctification; and that sanctification continues all through life. It is the growth in grace of a believer. But sanctification is never complete in this life. No man in this life ever attained to sinless perfection. It is the goal at which we aim, but we shall never reach it in this life. However, all God's people will reach the state of glory and perfection in the life to come.

So every true Christian is on a pilgrim journey. He is going from strength to strength, from one degree of grace to another. Indeed, says Paul, we are going 'from glory to glory, even as by the Spirit of the Lord' (2 Cor. 3:18).

The process whereby this is done is through Christ's intercession on our behalf to the Father and by the inward working of the Holy Spirit in our lives, especially through the Scriptures. 'Sanctify them through thy truth,' says Christ; 'thy word is truth' (John 17:17). So the principal means whereby God makes his people holy is the Bible and the preaching of the Bible. Our duty is to listen carefully to the word of God—the reading of it and especially the preaching of it. That is what preaching is for. It is for the conversion of men and the sanctification of converted men. It is in order to bring us on so that we do not remain forever babes in the faith but grow in knowledge, faith and every other grace. In that way we are daily prepared for glory.

That is why I bring to you this text. Here in this chapter of John we see Jesus Christ describing himself in these terms: 'I am the true vine, and my Father is the husbandman. Every branch in me that beareth not fruit he taketh away: and every branch that beareth fruit, he purgeth it [or pruneth it], that it may bring forth more fruit' (verses 1–2). If you are not a believer in Christ, you have not begun to be holy. It does not matter how decent your life or how moral your conduct, if you are not a believer in Christ you are unholy; your best works are abominable to God. Nothing you can do can possibly please God.

'Well,' you say to me, 'that's very severe. Why should that be?' The answer I give you is this: because until you come to faith in Christ you cannot please God, and you cannot begin to be holy. Holiness begins only when we come to faith in Jesus Christ the Son of God. That is one of the things which Christ is telling us here.

He says that he is the true vine and his people are the branches of the vine. As we all know, the nature of a tree, whether it be a vine or any other kind, is such that the sap flows from the root, up the trunk and into the branches, and gives life to the leaves and the fruit. As soon as you saw off a branch it ceases to make leaves or produce fruit. There is no sap reaching that part of the branch, and without the sap there cannot be life.

This is the illustration which Christ is setting before us here. If we are united to Christ by faith, then the sap—which is an illustration of the Holy Spirit—reaches to our soul, to our life, to our heart. The consequence is that we shall bring forth fruit. Indeed, our Lord puts it this way: 'As the branch cannot bear fruit of itself, except it abide in the vine; no more can ye, except ye abide in me. I am the vine, ye are the branches: he that abideth in me, and I in him, the same bringeth forth much fruit: for without me ye can do nothing' (verses 4–5).

Until you and I have come to Christ by faith, we have no life in us. And in so claiming to be the true vine, Christ is, of course, claiming to be the Son of God. He is asserting that he is unique, the only way to God; the only Saviour; the only conveyor of spiritual life. In John's Gospel Christ several times uses phrases beginning 'I am'. Then he follows with a comparison: 'I am the living bread'; 'I am the light of the world'; 'I am the good shepherd'; 'I am the true vine'; 'I am the way, the truth and the life'; and so on. All these assertions are affirmations of Christ's divinity; they claim equality with God. There is nothing less in these statements than that Jesus Christ is God. Unless we come to Christ by faith we have no part in his salvation.

Let us pause for a moment to ask ourselves, Have I come to faith in Christ? Do I know what it means to be united to Christ—to believe in him? Have I come to him as to the living God and Saviour of the world? Have I confessed my sins to him? Have I turned my back on the world? Have I taken up my cross and begun to follow him?

That is the way we must begin. If you can say 'yes' to these questions, you are in the happy position of being one of these branches in the vine. On the other hand, if you cannot genuinely say so, you have not even begun. You are still in your sins. You are under the judgment and condemnation of Almighty God. You are not on the way to heaven. I have to say to you in all solemnity that you are on the highway that leads to hell. And for that reason we are considering the most important subject in the world here. Baptism does not make us Christians; being born in a so-called Christian country does not make us Christians; being children of a Christian family does not make us Christians. Only as we come to Christ and believe in him as our own Saviour do we each one begin to have spiritual life. So we must put this question to ourselves first of all: Do I know what it is to have fellowship and communion with the Son of God? Let every man consult his own conscience before God in answering that question.

There is something in these words here which is rather puzzling. We find it in verse 2: 'Every branch in me that beareth not fruit he taketh away.' This is a very interesting statement which appears at first sight to be a contradiction. Christ speaks about a branch in him that beareth not fruit and is taken away.

How can a branch be in Christ and not bear fruit, and what is meant by its being taken away? He is referring here not to real Christians, but to nominal Christians. That is what he means by 'every branch in me': he refers to persons who claim to be Christians, but are not. How do we know they are not? They bear no fruit. Sooner or later, either in this life or at death, they will be removed. That is what we do in the garden. If one of the branches brings forth no fruit, the gardener comes and snips it off and throws it on the fire. So what our Lord means to tell us here is that if there is no fruit to the glory of God in our lives as professing Christians, then that is evidence of the fact that we are not real Christians but are merely nominal Christians. Every true and genuine believer brings forth the fruits of holiness and obedience to God's word.

Sometimes people know a great deal of the Bible, but they say in their heart of hearts, 'I don't want to be too strict; I don't want to be too careful in keeping the commandments of God. Why should I do all these things? It is not fashionable.' It could be that you have got into a slipshod state of mind. 'Oh,' you say, 'I believe in Christ. He is my Saviour.' 'All right,' I say, 'is there any fruit in your life? Is there any godliness in your life? Is there a careful keeping of the word of God? Do you read the Bible, not simply by moving the marker from day to day, but because you want to live for the glory of God?' Here is the test. If you desire thoroughly and conscientiously to obey the word of God, then that is a hopeful sign that you have come to the knowledge of salvation.

On the other hand, you might say, 'Well, I'm not going to go as far with my obedience as I see some other people go; I don't like all this talk about strictness, carefulness and obedience. I am here to enjoy myself'; or, 'My life is my own; why should I subject myself to things that I don't like? I want to get the most out of this life. I want to please myself.' If we talk like that, it shows that we are probably only professing Christians and nothing more. We have some sort of faith in our head, but not the reality of that faith in our heart.

The evidence of faith in our heart is that we bring forth and bear fruit to the glory of God. Ask yourself how you stand.

In Britain we get apples from Australia, New Zealand, Canada, and so on. They are stamped 'Class A' or 'Class B'. Class A apples are expensive but very good. Class B are not so good and not so big. And so on, down the list. So would you say about yourself that you are Class A in fruitfulness, or Class B, or Class C? Where do you come?

But listen to Christ: 'Herein is my Father glorified, that ye bear much fruit.' The purpose of life for a Christian is not so much what you can get out of it, not your own happiness nor your own pleasure, but how much you live to the glory of God. 'Man's chief end is to glorify God and to enjoy him for ever.' Let a man examine himself, therefore, in the light of these things and consider how to improve.

You are to become more obedient and more genuine in your following of Christ than you have been. You will never regret it, because the holier you are, the happier you will be. Happiness is linked with holiness. Happiness is a by-product of holiness; and the more godly—the more holy—a person is, the happier he will be.

God is perfectly happy because he is perfectly holy; and the angels are perfectly happy because they are perfectly holy. The saints in glory are perfectly happy after death because they are now perfectly holy.

The unhappiness of this world arises from its unholiness; and the more unholy people become, the more unhappy they will be, sooner or later. This is sadly true of the Hollywood film stars. If we live after the flesh we shall reap the things of the flesh; and if we live after the Spirit—the things of God—we shall reap the things of the Spirit of God. There is no happiness without holiness; and holiness begins when we come to be united to Christ.

So Jesus says, 'I am the true vine … every branch that beareth fruit, he purgeth it, that it may bring forth more fruit' (verses 1–2). When a branch is fruitful the gardener comes with his pruning knife and cuts out extraneous twigs here and there in order that the branch may bring forth more fruit. The gardener knows his work. He is trained to do it. Next season round, the branch that bore ten apples now brings forth twenty-four; and the following year, forty-eight. The branch is becoming more fruitful season by season.

That is a picture of God's dealings in the life of a believer. God takes out the sharp knife of his discipline and he cuts away from our lives those things which are no help to us. In the course of cutting away the things that are unfruitful, he makes us more useful, more spiritual, more godly than we were before.

In the course of doing this the Lord may have to hurt us. To have him cut into our lives with the sharp knife of his discipline is painful. We may well cry out to God against it. But God knows better than we do. And the way of holiness involves submitting ourselves to the teaching of God's word and to the providential discipline and chastening which he sends.

Has God been dealing with you? Has God been interfering in your life for the better? Have you felt the sharp knife of his pruning? Is God removing from your life those things which are no help to you? Has he been showing you, for instance, that there is no point at all in wasting time with worthless programmes and mindless popular music? Has God been pointing out to you that that is a source of unfruitfulness in your life and that it is not going to lead to more spirituality? Such things will not help you to bring forth fruit to the glory of God.

Let us say a little more now about our union with Christ. In the Bible, we come across three great unions. There is the union between the Father, the Son and the Holy Spirit. This is the union of the Persons of the Godhead.

Then there is another union mentioned in Scripture: that of the two natures in Christ. Christ is the eternal Son of God; but he became man by taking our nature to himself. He became both God and man, two natures and yet one person. There are not two Christs; there is but one Christ. The two natures in Christ are distinct within the one person. Christ has two minds. He has two wills. We refer to this union of two natures in Christ as the 'hypostatic' union.

But then there is a third union, and it is this union that Christ is referring to here in John 15. It is called the 'mystical' union. It is the union of believers with Christ. Christ is united to all believers, and all believers are united to him. This union between believers in Christ is a far closer and more intimate relationship than that between natural members of a family.

In the New Testament this doctrine of the unity of believers with Christ is expressed in various ways. In one illustration Paul refers to Christ as the head and his people as the body, the members. That is one of the indications that Christ and believers belong together in the one body. As the head controls the body, so Christ, in glory, controls all Christians. We are under him. He dictates the terms upon which we have fellowship with him. He is our government, our prime minister, our sole head and authority. That means that we are dependent upon Christ for all our knowledge of how to do what is right. Christ tells us this in the Bible. We might ask ourselves: Are we living in union with Christ in such a way that whatever he says in his word, we are doing it?

We have no right to do anything but what the Head of the church tells us to do. You see how relevant this is to modern life. Take the whole question of women in the ministry and women elders in the church. All we need to do to solve the question is to ask, What has Christ—our intelligence—told us? And it is all here in his word.

Take another example, the whole issue of whether Protestant churches should unite with the Church of Rome. It is a very relevant subject. Is there any harm in Protestant churches' uniting with the Church of Rome? After all, they say they are Christians and we are Christians, so what is the harm? What we need to do is to read, study and find out what Christ, who is our 'intelligence' in heaven, is saying in this Book, and we have the answer. We do not have to do our own independent thinking. We do not have to be 'up to date' with our own theories. Christ is our 'brain'; he is our Head. Therefore we are obliged to do what he tells us to do. The Church of Rome is doctrinally very far removed from the Bible, so no Protestant should unite with it.

Another illustration of our union with Christ is this: the building and its foundation. The New Testament says that Christ is the foundation stone. 'Other foundation can no man lay than that is laid, which is Jesus Christ' (1 Cor. 3:11). His church is built upon this foundation.

Then there is this further illustration: we are said as believers to be married to Christ. Marriage is used as an illustration of our union with Christ so that when we come to faith in him we are not our own. Christ is our husband; we are his bride. When you come to Christ and believe in him and become his bride you must take Christ for better or for worse, in sickness and in health, till you come to the end of life. When you are a single person you are free; but when you come to marriage you are not free. When you come to Christ you have a Husband who tells you that you must be faithful to him in all things, and if your eyes stray after worldly pleasure and worldly lust it is a sign that you are committing spiritual fornication. You are being untrue to your Husband and unfaithful to your Lord. You are forgetting that when you took Christ as your Saviour, you took him for better or worse (it is impossible to take Christ for worse, but I am using human speech to make the point).

What, then, is the nature of this union with Christ? First of all, it is an invisible union; and, secondly, it is spiritual. It is a spiritual relationship between believers and Christ the mediator. This union with Christ is maintained in two ways. On our part it is maintained by faith; and on his part it is maintained by the Holy Spirit in our hearts. There is a two-way relationship between Christ and his people. We, for our part, must believe in him and trust him. He is our Lord and we are united to him by faith, so we must trust him implicitly. Perhaps you say, 'That's easy.' I am afraid it is not! It takes a whole lifetime to learn how to trust Christ as we ought to do.

Do the right thing and he will never let you down. Obey him and take him at his word. He is united to you; you are united to him.

'Ah,' you say, 'I may not have the courage or the strength. I may fail.' Of course you may, but it is not only our faith that unites us to Christ; it is his Holy Spirit. We are united to Christ by the Spirit. Christ dwells in us by his Spirit. That is why the Apostle Paul could say, 'I can do all things through Christ which strengtheneth me' (Phil. 4:13). Is that your view of life? Is that the way in which you face the difficulties of life from day to day? It should be if you are a professing Christian.

So this union is invisible and spiritual, yet real. And once you come to faith in Christ you become united to him for ever. It is a union that nothing can break, not even death. The body is still united to Christ, still belongs to Christ, even in death. And when the trumpet sounds at the end of the world and the dead are raised, the body will come out of the grave in glory. It will shine with radiance like that of Christ himself because the body belongs to the Lord. We belong to him in life and in death. He will own us as his own people. Hence we are united to our Lord and Saviour not only in this life but after death, and then in eternity beyond the judgment day, world without end.

Here is the wonder of our condition as believers. It is not as though Christ has just saved us and left us to get on with things; he has saved us to take us to glory. He has purchased us by his death. He has paid the ransom to the justice of God so that our sins, which are many, may be pardoned. We are admitted freely into the audience of God in prayer in this life, and at last our persons, body and soul, will be admitted into his presence.

Hence it is that the Bible tells us of a 'mystery'. 'We shall not all sleep, but we shall all be changed, in a moment, in the twinkling of an eye, at the last trump: for the trumpet shall sound, and the dead shall be raised incorruptible, and we shall be changed. For this corruptible must put on incorruption, and this mortal must put on immortality' (1 Cor. 15:51–3).

The day will soon arrive for every Christian when he will leave behind him his weak and frail body in the earth, and his soul will go to be with God and with Christ. It cannot be otherwise because we are united to him. He is our Head and we are the members of his mystical body. All God's people will meet together at last.

There is one further thing to say: the Bible talks not only about having union with Christ, but also of communion with him. Christ says, 'If ye keep my commandments, ye shall abide in my love; even as I have kept my Father's commandments, and abide in his love' (verse 10). Here our Lord goes beyond what he has just said. In the early part of John

15 Christ talks about abiding in him. But from verse 10 he goes beyond that and speaks about abiding in his love. We must not miss the distinction.

Abiding in Christ is union with him, and abiding in Christ's love is communion with him. Let me illustrate the point. When two persons who are married have a disagreement, it does not dissolve the tie of marriage, but it does spoil the fellowship between them for a time. So between the believer and Christ, the union is not broken when we fall into sin, but the communion is broken. Union is something which is always there; communion is something which is consciously enjoyed by fellowship.

As Christians, we are united to Christ always. Nothing that happens can ever break that union. He will never divorce us. He keeps his word: 'I will betroth thee unto me for ever' (Hos. 2:19). If as a Christian I begin to do wrong things, I will not be divorced by Christ. The union will never be broken; but something will be broken. It is the communion: Christ will be displeased with me if I do something wrong, and he will withdraw something of his blessing from my heart. I cannot tell you what that means altogether, but it is as though a shadow falls over your life. When we sin against him and disobey him he may well withdraw the light of his countenance for a time so that we feel the shadow of his disapproval.

That does not mean to say we are no longer Christians. We are still united to him. But something has been broken for a time, something is lost, and that is the enjoyment of his love. 'Continue ye in my love. If ye keep my commandments, ye shall abide in my love' (verses 9–10).

Why are there so many Christians in this world who are half-hearted in their love of Christ? It is no doubt partly because they are living in disobedience to his word and are not enjoying more of his love. They are walking at a distance. It was so with Simon Peter. He ceased to enjoy the love of Christ for a time because he was living at a distance; he was following afar off and he denied his Lord.

The lesson is obvious for us: if we want to enjoy Christ's love we must do what he tells us to do. We must find out his will from the Bible. If we want much of his love, we must give him a whole-hearted, full-hearted, sincere obedience. This is not perfection; we shall never have that in this world. But he does expect us to walk obediently. After all, he died for you and me; and he tells us here in John 15: 'You are my friends. I have died for you. And greater love hath no man than this, that a man should lay down his life for his friends.' And as you and I face the Saviour in his word, we have to say to him, 'O Lord, I have been a very poor friend, and I have often disobeyed thee; but O, blessed Christ, I come to thee and I humbly ask for forgiveness that I have not been a better, more obedient disciple. O Lord, I realize that I have not honoured thee as I should have done. I have not brought forth fruit for the glory of God as I should have done. But I ask thee, O Lord, to change my life and to make me one of those branches that abide in the vine. Oh, may I bring forth much fruit to the glory and praise of God. Give me a full taste of thy love and teach me to hold frequent communion with thee in this life. Amen.'

SEVEN

Glory in Prospect

Nay, in all these things we are more than conquerors through him that loved us.—Rom. 8:37.

These, obviously, are glorious words—and as we learn catechisms, so too we must learn texts. You could not do your soul a better service than to learn this text here and to commit it to your memory, to inscribe it on the tables of your heart. We ought to cherish these glorious words to our dying day.

These words are, of course, addressed not to all mankind, but to Christians who are now being sanctified and who at last will be glorified.

It is a strange fact that the Christian who has the hope of glory is often found in this life to be afraid. On the other hand, the worldly man, who has no hope of glory, is occasionally over-confident, even at times when facing death. The reason for this strange situation is that the worldly man does not realize what will happen to him when he dies. He does not believe that God will cast him into the lake of fire and brimstone. So he goes on towards the precipice of eternal destruction as a blind man staggers towards the edge of a cliff, not knowing that the next step will carry him to his eternal ruin.

The Christian, by contrast, is one who *does* know the seriousness of dying. He appreciates the solemnities associated with death. It is this knowledge of eternal things that leaves him deeply concerned in case he should be a castaway.

There are some Christians who, sadly, do not understand that once we are converted we are safe for ever. There are Christians who have wrongly taken the view that you can be saved and then lost; that you can be converted and then totally fall away.

I remember some years ago meeting a girl whose upbringing was with a very Arminian group of Christians. I heard her say, 'We don't believe that Christians will persevere. We believe you can be saved on a Monday, lost on a Tuesday, restored on a Wednesday and fall again on a Thursday'—or words to that effect. Happily, that is not the teaching of the word of God. If we are converted, we can never fully or finally fall away. So let us remove from our minds any possibility that if we have come to Christ we could be lost.

However, there is another reason why some Christians entertain fear concerning the future. It is because of their own temperament. We are all different in our temperament, just as we are different in other respects. Some Christians are naturally gloomy, melancholy and fearful. The temperament of some is such that they dare not allow themselves to rejoice in hope of the coming glory. They hide in the shadows because of their own timidity.

Again, there are some Christians who have assurance for a time, but then lose it owing to temptation, sin or difficulty of one kind or another. Mercifully, we do not need assurance to get to heaven. We are not saved by assurance; we are saved by faith. Just as we do not need a birth certificate to prove that we are alive, so we do not need assurance to get to heaven. However, strong assurance gives the Christian great strength and comfort along the way. The Christian will only go limping to heaven without assurance.

So the Bible gives us large measures of comfort. It everywhere assures us that we shall be preserved by the power of God unto eternal glory.

No passage of the Bible assures us more powerfully or more eloquently than the end of Romans 8. Here the Apostle Paul tells us of his persuasion that nothing shall separate us from the love of Christ. God will receive us into his nearer presence at last.

I want to look at this because it is very closely connected with our theme of sanctification and glorification. The words of verse 37 are our text: 'Nay, in all these things we are more than conquerors through him that loved us.'

First of all, he is speaking here about the believer and the believer's being more than a conqueror. That is a very arresting phrase. We are familiar with the idea of people conquering in battle; but to be more than a conqueror sounds a very exaggerated expression. The original word used here by the Apostle Paul is of special interest. It could be translated 'hyper-conqueror'. The word *hyper* in Greek means 'over and above the normal'. We have 'hypermarkets' in our day. The old markets were tucked away in a corner of the town, probably not the most important part, but now the 'hypermarkets'—huge malls, as Americans call them—are filled with all kinds of shops, stores and apartments.

That is the idea behind this word 'more than conquerors'—'hyper-conquerors'. We are conquerors not simply on an ordinary scale, but on a great scale. That is the phrase the Apostle Paul uses, and in order to show the reality of this fact that we are, as Christians, more than conquerors he piles up a heap of arguments one on top of another. In this way Paul reassures us that we may be *certain* that God will receive us into glory at last. We shall not only be conquerors over death, tribulation and the devil; we shall be *more* than conquerors.

What is Paul telling us? I think first of all we could say this: the believer knows what his end and destiny is. We do not know as Christians *when* we shall die, and we do not know as Christians *how* we shall die—what a mercy! But we do know that when we die we shall be with God and with Christ in glory. We shall shine in glory; we shall be with the Lord Jesus Christ who died for us. We know that we shall be with all those who truly love God. 'There remaineth … a rest to the people of God' (Heb. 4:9). This is the saints' everlasting rest, a place where we shall be at home with God.

We know what our end will be. That is a great thing because the world does not know what its end will be. They may have pleasure today, money in the bank and all manner of good things which they eat, drink and share among themselves in this life, but as soon as godless men and women come to death, *all* their good things pass away for ever. When the wicked come to the point of death they are stripped naked of everything that can give them pleasure. They are plunged at once into outer darkness, where 'their worm dieth not, and the fire is not quenched' (Mark 9:44). They are cast into the lake of fire and brimstone with the devil and his angels, and there they are locked in chains awaiting the judgment day.

This is why we must tell sinners of their urgent need to repent and believe the gospel, lest they come to that fearful condition of being eternally cast away from God. There is no second chance after death. There is no 'love of God deeper than hell', as some theologians have tried to pretend. No—our only hope is in this life.

If you are not a true Christian, I have to say to you that only in this life have you the hope of getting right with God. If you should happen to be travelling home and have an accident and your life is cut off, there is no more gospel for you—no more church, no more preaching, no more praying, no more hope, but only misery without any end. A million years of misery is but the beginning of it; there are another million to follow—indeed, an unbroken eternity of sorrow for those who do not know Christ. What I have said is solemn, but it is only a shadow of the reality, and I beg you, therefore, if you are not a Christian, to think about and to understand the true condition of your soul. You need to plead with God for mercy. You need to pray for deliverance from the wrath and curse which are to come upon all the souls of godless men when they die.

But the Christian, on the other hand, is in exactly the opposite condition. The Christian is in the happy and blessed state of knowing that when he dies he is going to be with the Lord. It will be well with his soul.

Let us remember to take these thoughts with us when we read good books that remind us of the courage of our forefathers. The gospel which we have in our countries was very dearly bought with the labours and blood of Reformers, Puritans and Covenanters. Great Christians in the past gave their lives that you and I today might have a Bible in our own language. That is a great privilege. They do not have that in North Korea, China or in some African countries. But we have it. We owe it to God's mercy and to the sufferings of men and women before us that we have these things, and we must make sure that we value them.

Now, the believer knows in his warfare in this life what worldly men do not know in their warfare in this life. When men go to war they do not know what the outcome of that war will be. For example, some of us are old enough to remember the Second World War. When Adolph Hitler and the Nazis went to war against other nations, he had no idea whether he would be victorious or not. He thought he would be. He had his soldiers, his airports, his navy, his submarines, and so on. He hoped he would conquer the world, but he did not. He did not know what the outcome was going to be. The final end was that he shot himself—or was shot—in his own bunker, unhappy man.

Hitler had no idea when he went to war whether he would win or not. But the Christian knows, even before he comes to the great conflict with death, what the issue of his warfare will be! We know as Christians that we shall be more than conquerors over all our enemies.

We are *more than conquerors* because when the end of the battle comes not a single one of our enemies will be left standing. The devil will be cast out finally into his eternal place of doom. He will never tempt us any more. The wicked who have hated the church and persecuted God's people will be cast out. Not one of them will ever vex or trouble the people of God any more. Death itself, which is the last enemy, will be destroyed. There will be no more death. Death will be swallowed up of life. Death will be behind the people of God for ever.

Even before we come to death, or judgment, we know that we are more than conquerors already, that we are to be victorious over all our enemies. None of them will stand in the end, but we will have the victory over them all.

Then also we know that not one of those defeated enemies will, in the end of the day, rise up to trouble us a second time. People thought that the First World War was 'the war to end all wars', but the enemy rose up a second time. He had been defeated, but he came back, in 1939–45. But the Christian will be more than a conqueror in this sense also: that all his enemies will be utterly defeated in the end.

There will be no second rebellion of the devil and his angels. There will be no second fall of Adam. Adam's children, as many of them as are redeemed in that day, will all be safe; and we shall be so safe in heaven as never to be able to sin again. Adam was made perfect, but his perfection was mutable. He could lose it. But in heaven the saints of God will be so immutably holy that they will be beyond the possibility of ever sinning any more. They will be more than conquerors over death, and over sin. They are more than conquerors when they come to the end of their conflict.

Furthermore, the Christian knows before he comes to his final end and to glory that he is more than a conqueror in this further sense: whereas all our enemies will be defeated, none of our brethren in Christ will be lost. Not one of the Lord's people will be lost. All the church will be saved. That is extraordinary. When did you ever hear of a war in which all the adversaries were destroyed, but not a single soldier was overthrown on your side?

Usually in battle, thousands are lost on both sides, and only after terrible bloodshed and conflict does one side overcome the other. But in this battle of heavenly powers against the powers of evil we know that we are more than conquerors in that not a single one of the army of Christ will ever be lost. We shall all get safe to glory. Not a single one will be missing. Every man, woman and child whose name is in the Book of Life will most assuredly come to that glorious salvation promised for us in Holy Scripture.

No wonder, then, the word of God tells us that we are more than conquerors! No wonder the Bible says we are super-conquerors, hyper- conquerors, overwhelmingly conquerors!

Christian, rejoice as you go to heaven. Do not hang down your head in defeat; do not allow your fears to overwhelm you. You are a child of the living God. You are one of those who is honourable in the annals of heaven. You are chosen to be one of his peculiar people! Rejoice!

Our victory, our success in battle, is not to be ascribed to anything that we are or can do. It is all attributable to God. Paul says that it is due to the one who loved us. Paul here refers to the triune and blessed God. He has just said, 'If God be for us, who can be against us?' (verse 31). All our successes come from God alone. And he tells us that God loves us. We are more than conquerors through this loving God.

God is a Holy Trinity—the Father, the Son and the Holy Spirit. Each of these three divine Persons loves us as Christians. Each one loves us infinitely. Each one loved us eternally before we were born.

That is how we became Christians. We did not become Christians by our own free will, but by his sovereign will; not by our power, but by his grace. He loved us eternally, and so his Spirit operated in our lives and brought us to and gave us this faith. So, says Paul, it is the love of God and the God of love who secures this victory for us. It is given the title of a 'hyper-victory'. It is a 'super' victory, a 'total' victory, an entire and complete victory over all those who hate us in this present age. So our victory is attributed to the love of each divine Person.

The Father is for us; the Son is for us; and the Spirit is for us. What does that mean? How is the Holy Spirit for us? In what sense? It was the Holy Spirit who gave to us our new birth. We were born again through the Spirit of God. That was what Jesus said to Nicodemus in John 3: 'You must be born of water and of the Spirit.' Here 'water' does not refer to baptism but to the cleansing power of the blood of Christ applied to the soul by the Holy Spirit. It is the effectual working of God's Spirit in the hearts of sinners which makes them clean and pure.

The late Professor John Murray of Westminster Seminary in the USA once put it memorably like this: 'You don't usually go to the aristocracy to get your dirty jobs done.' He then hastened to say that there is no dishonour in having to do dirty jobs; there is no shame in being a charwoman, a cleaner of a building or a sweeper of streets. These are honourable jobs. But then he added, 'You do not usually get your street cleaners, your char-ladies and your other cleaners from the aristocracy. You usually get them from people in humble walks of life.' 'But,' said Murray, 'the dirtiest work in the world is done by a most exalted Person—the Holy Spirit. He came into your heart and into mine; into these hearts of ours which are like a running sewer of defilement. This Holy Spirit came into the heart and he cleansed the heart.'

Not only that, but he condescends to dwell in our heart all the days of our life in this world. What is he doing? Cleansing, sanctifying, purifying our lives. What love!

Surely this is unsurpassed love. And that is what the Apostle Paul means. We are more than conquerors because the Holy Spirit loved us, loves us still, and goes on helping us in this work of sanctification.

But then also he says that the Father loves us. How does the Father love us? Paul has told us this in verses 28–30: 'All things work together for good to them that love God, to them who are the called according to his purpose. For whom he did foreknow, he also did predestinate to be conformed to the image of his Son, that he might be the first-born among many brethren. Moreover whom he did predestinate, them he also called: and whom he called, them he also justified: and whom he justified, them he also glorified.'

He is telling us here about the love which the Father has towards us, and how that love is explained. Before there was a universe, God the Father conceived a plan. He foreknew his people—which is another way of saying that he loved them. He chose them, he picked them out. The English word 'foreknow' is not so clear, but that is the way that the writers of the Bible express the idea. It is selection: God chose a people out for himself. He loved them, not for any good in them or because they were better than others, but because it was his good pleasure to love them and choose them for his own sake. Having loved them, he then predestinated them. He so arranged everything in life that they would infallibly come to Christ and be converted. They did not know this when they were living in this world. But God's predestination guaranteed that sooner or later they would come to Christ.

The elect are guaranteed to come to salvation. Those who are predestinated he also calls. This is what we term 'effectual calling'. It is the hearing of God's voice in the gospel. When people hear preaching, some never hear anything except the voice of the preacher. But those whom God loves, who are in the purpose, hear more than that: they hear the *inward* call of God. Have you heard the voice of God? Do you know what it is for the Almighty to be speaking to you? Or do you just hear the preacher? If you have heard God's voice you will know the difference because you will be changed.

Then those whom God calls he justifies; that is to say, they come to the state in which God says that they are not guilty. They are not under condemnation. Their faith in Christ has saved them from the curse of the law. Their faith is counted for righteousness. They are saved and are safe. And those whom God justifies he also glorifies.

The purpose of God, then, consists of these five golden 'links': foreknowledge, predestination, calling, justification, glorification. God's plan cannot be overthrown. All those whom he loves he will certainly bring to faith, to Christ and to heaven. Undergirding us and on either side of us is the eternal purpose. From everlasting to everlasting, the mercy of the Lord is upon them that fear him, and his righteousness is unto children's children. Oh, the loving Father and the loving Spirit!

But what about the Son? 'We are more than conquerors through him that loved us.' What has the Son done for us? Paul asks certain rhetorical questions at the end of this chapter which make this clear: 'He that spared not his own Son, but delivered him up for us all, how shall he not with him also freely give us all things?' (verse 32). The argument is this: God has sent his Son into the world. Jesus came to the cross to bear our sins; and when Jesus was in the garden of Gethsemane he said, 'O my Father, if it be possible, let this cup pass from me' (Matt. 26:39). The 'cup' referred to the cross.

Jesus later exclaimed, 'The cup which my Father hath given me, shall I not drink it?' (John 18:11). He had earlier said, 'I have a baptism to be baptized with; and how am I straitened till it be accomplished!' (Luke 12:50). Christ longed to get to the cross because of the love he bore to us. 'The good shepherd giveth his life for the sheep' (John 10:11). Christ, the Son, gave himself for his people, sealing up the eternal covenant and purpose of God with the blood of the everlasting covenant. He sealed it by his own death. By dying for us he made sure that all the people of God would get safely home to glory.

Then the apostle asks other questions: 'Who shall lay any thing to the charge of God's elect?' (verse 33). Paul means that many evil forces will try to stop us getting to heaven. Paul envisages Satan coming and standing before God and saying, 'But these people are all sinners. They do not deserve to get to heaven.' These powers of evil that assemble before God's throne accuse us, saying, 'Believers have no right to get to heaven! They're all sinners!' But Paul replies, to comfort us, 'Who is he that condemneth? It is Christ that died' (verse 34); 'it is God that justifieth' (verse 33).

God will not accept any accusation against his own people. Christ has died for them. 'They are not going to be condemned by anyone,' says God. 'I am their justifier.' It is because Christ has loved them. We are more than conquerors through him that loved us.

The love of the Spirit, the love of the Father and the love of the Son are clearly shown in the eternal plan. And Christ is risen again and is even at the right hand of God. He also makes intercession for us.

By telling us these things Paul means us to be strengthened. The love of Christ, he says, is wonderfully comforting.

He died for us! But that is only a part of it. Christ rose again, and shows the universe that the atonement was accepted by God. If the atonement for our sins had not been sufficient, God would not have accepted it and he would not have raised Christ from the dead. The raising of Christ from the dead is the proof that God was pleased to accept his offering for us. His death was a substitutionary sacrifice.

What else? Christ, having risen, is today at the right hand of God. There he appears, bearing our names upon the palms of his hands. He bears our names before the Father. And he makes intercession for us.

So I want to reassure you that you and I today are more than conquerors—hyper-conquerors—because we have this loving God, this Trinity, with us and for us. But I close with two questions.

Christian friend, in the light of this, do you not see how assured you should be? 'Oh,' you say, 'for a moment I was afraid of death, but I am not afraid now. I am coming home to God. I am coming home to my Father and to my Saviour. Death, for me, is coming home to Christ.' Yes, that is the way to look at it. It is a coming home to this loving God. When that happens he will wipe away all tears from our eyes. All the angels of God will sound their praises when they see us get there because we are more than conquerors through him who loved us.

But what about you who are not Christians? I am afraid I cannot give you any of this comfort. This comfort is for the children of God. I would be a deceiver if I pretended that any of this comfort is for you. Not until you come to believe in Christ for yourself may you have this comfort. But when you have trusted Jesus as your Lord, then everything the Bible says will be for your personal reassurance too. So, if you never did so before, now is the golden moment when you must say to Christ, 'My Lord and my God!'

I can reassure you that you will be welcomed by God because his arms of grace are stretched out to receive penitent sinners. 'Come,' says God. 'And whosoever will, let him take the water of life freely' (Rev. 22:17).

EIGHT

The Groaning Creation

For the earnest expectation of the creature waiteth for the manifestation of the sons of God. For the creature was made subject to vanity, not willingly, but by reason of him who hath subjected the same in hope, Because the creature itself also shall be delivered from the bondage of corruption into the glorious liberty of the children of God. For we know that the whole creation groaneth and travaileth in pain together until now. And not only they, but ourselves also, which have the firstfruits of the Spirit, even we ourselves groan within ourselves, waiting for the adoption, to wit, the redemption of our body.—Rom. 8:19–23.

In these words the Apostle Paul is speaking of the great change which is to come to Christians and to the whole universe at the end of the world. In this present age Christians must needs suffer in many ways, and he refers to that in verse 18 when he says that 'the sufferings of this present time are not worthy to be compared with the glory which shall be revealed in us'.

Our theme has been that of sanctification and glorification. The two come together in that single verse. Paul explains that in this life the Lord's people must be content to suffer for a little time. They suffer rejection by the world; they suffer misunderstanding from unbelievers; and they suffer in many other respects here in this present age. But the glory which is to be revealed in us at the end of the world is so incalculably great, he says, that there is no comparison between our present sufferings and the glory hereafter. Our sufferings are but a trifle, hardly worth the noticing, compared with the glory of God which is to be revealed in us and in the universe of which the Lord's people will be the heirs. The Bible tells us that the saints are to inherit a new heaven and a new earth. So we come in this final section to look at what God tells us here concerning the glory which is to be when Christ returns.

Very often the Lord's people feel a sense of loneliness and isolation here in this world. It is a common experience. It is as though in this life the Lord's people feel themselves to be nobodies. They do not normally get into the headlines; they are not mentioned by the media. It is other people who are spoken of most often. The Lord's people are marginalized. They are set on the edge of the stage as those who do not count. But the teaching of this part of Scripture is that, as Christians, we are not so lonely as we may suppose.

Notice that at verse 19 Paul says, 'The earnest expectation of the creature waiteth for the manifestation of the sons of God.' What does he mean by 'the creature', or 'the creation'? Let us look at it negatively first. It is very obvious that he is not referring to sinners, to the unbelieving world, in this verse. We know that that is the case because the unbelieving world is not interested in the manifestation of the sons of God. The world outside of Christ has not the remotest interest in the destiny of Christians.

Secondly, he cannot here be referring to angels, because angels have not been subject to bondage, which is what he says is true of this 'creature'. He says that the creature that longs for the manifestation of the sons of God is a creature that shall be delivered from the bondage of corruption (verse 21); and that cannot refer to angels for the very obvious reason that angels were never subject to vanity. Angels never sinned; they are not in a condition of being subjected to this corruption.

Then, thirdly, he cannot here be referring to devils, because the devils are not going to be delivered from their bondage (verse 21). The devils were cast out of heaven when they sinned, and they are now kept under chains in darkness, waiting for the judgment of the great day.

So what does the apostle mean by 'the creature' in verse 19? The only answer we can give is that it is the universe round about us—the material universe; the sun, moon and stars, and the earth beneath us. It is the world in which we live—not the rational part, but the material part. Paul is using a very strong figure of speech. He says it is as though the sun, moon, stars and earth are at this time taking an interest in the future destiny of the people of God. The way he puts that is very interesting: 'The creature waiteth for the manifestation of the sons of God.'

Let me say a little word about the expression 'the earnest expectation of the creature'. It describes something like what you do when you cannot see very clearly: you stand on tiptoe and you crane your neck to see. The picture is that of, let us say, a sporting event where a small boy is at the back of a crowd of adults. He cannot see what is happening on the playing field, so he hoists himself up on a box and then peers over the shoulders of those who are in front of him. The picture, therefore, which the Apostle Paul is giving us here is that all the universe round about us is looking down upon the Christians who are living in this world. It is looking down with the deepest concentration, and with the deepest interest, because the universe round about us longs to see the manifestation of the sons of God. I shall tell you what that is in just a moment, but let us realize that all eyes are upon us. Sun, moon, stars, universe—what are they waiting for? What are they peering to see? It is this: the day when Christians will appear in all their final, heavenly beauty.

We must go back to the beginning of history to explain what it is that the Bible teaches concerning the destiny of Christians. You may know the well-known book written by Thomas Boston, the Scottish writer of the eighteenth century, entitled *The Four-fold State of Man*—one of the best of Boston's writings. Notice that phrase 'the four-fold state of man'. Boston's teaching, which is thoroughly biblical, is that in the beginning God made man sinless. Man at first was in a state of innocence. But Adam sinned against God; and when Adam sinned, we, his children, sinned in him and fell with him from a state of innocence into a state of sin. That is the plight and the tragedy of the world. The entire world has been marred by sin. We see that every day we live. What beautiful countries God has made! South Africa, Sri Lanka, Ireland—yes, but they are spoiled by sin, with people killing one another. Something has gone terribly wrong! It is because man is in a state, a condition, of sin and evil. That is the second state of man.

But there is a third condition in which mankind can be, and that is the state of grace. This is what happens to us when we come to faith in Christ. We are delivered from the state of sin and brought into a state of redemption, a state of grace, through faith in Christ. All true Christians are in a state of grace. They are not yet perfect, but they are not in a state of sin. They are under the control and power of the Holy Spirit. They are renewed in their whole natures by the power of God. Basically, they love God. Fundamentally, they trust in God and they are different from others. It is not simply that Christians have believed a set of doctrines which has changed their thinking; no, conversion changes everything in man! It changes his mind, his will, his emotions, his conscience, his expectations, his ambitions—his everything! He is now delivered from a state of sin.

But there is a fourth state, still in the future: the state of glory. When Jesus Christ our Saviour, who is now at the right hand of God, returns at the end of history, he will glorify his people. Christ will stand upon the clouds and every eye will see him; and the nations of the world will groan, and seek to hide themselves under the rocks, in the caves and under the mountains. They will say to the rocks and the mountains, 'Fall on us, and hide us from the face of him that sitteth on the throne, and from the wrath of the Lamb: for the great day of his wrath is come; and who shall be able to stand?' (Rev. 6:16–17). That is how the unbelieving world will be at the end of history. They will be terrified to see Christ coming down to judge the world. Christ will then bring down the curtain, if you like, upon everything that has happened in the history of the world.

But when Christ comes at the end, Christians, so very far from having anything to be afraid of, will be changed. The bodies of believers will then in an instant be made full of glory. We will be glorified. It will be like turning on an electric light. When not switched on, it looks very dull. But it becomes suddenly bright and radiant as soon as the electricity is turned on. So it will be with the bodies of all Christians in the end.

These frail bodies are going to be transformed by the working of God's creative power, and he will fill them with glory and fit them for their heavenly condition. The Apostle Paul puts it like this: our bodies are sown in weakness and raised in power; they are sown in dishonour and raised in glory, in a moment, in the twinkling of an eye, at the last trumpet. 'The trumpet shall sound, and the dead shall be raised incorruptible, and we shall be changed' (1 Cor. 15:43, 52). This is the hope of the Christian, the destiny of all who love Jesus Christ. And by 'the earnest expectation of the creature', the apostle means that the universe is looking for this great event.

Suppose you are walking down the street. As you walk along the footpath you come to a church. There are people standing in front of the porch or main door of the church. You pause to look. Some of the people have cameras. They are all very happy. They are obviously at a wedding. Where is the bride? She is not outside yet. Where is the groom? He is not outside yet either. They are inside, and all these people are waiting with their cameras until the happy moment when the bride and groom stand in the porch. Then the cameras will click and everybody will be delighted because the happy moment has arrived.

Now, in a much higher sense, that is what the apostle is meaning here. It is as though the sun, the moon, the stars, the earth, indeed the entire universe round about us, is like a massive crowd of spectators. They are all craning their necks to see something. They are waiting for the bride and the bridegroom to appear. What do I mean? They are waiting for the marriage of Christ and the church. They are waiting for the day when the happy pair—if I may put it that way—are united together in indissoluble glory; because when Christ appears in the clouds of heaven his church will be gathered up into the air to meet him and to be united with him in glory. The universe knows that and is now waiting for it.

I have to stop and say that it does not look like that, does it? It seems to us with the eye of sense as though that will never happen. It seems as though the Christian faith is getting weaker and weaker. Where are the glorious days of the past? Where are the glorious revivals which our fathers saw? It is as though all the promises of God are asleep.

But by faith we know that this is not so. We understand that the day is going to come when all the promises of God will suddenly spring to life. Everything that God has promised will then come to pass. The whole creation knows very well that what God has said will and must happen. Christ and his bride will appear upon the stage of history at the end and they will be united in marriage for ever. Because of that, the whole universe is now waiting.

This is a dreary world for Christians to go through. We have so many disappointments and we are aware of such a long waiting time. How long have you been a Christian? 'Oh,' says one, 'twenty years.' 'Thirty-five years,' says somebody else. 'Fifty years,' says an older person, 'and I've been waiting all these years to be married to Christ in the glory, and still I'm waiting.' But let me comfort you. Do you know how long the sun and the moon have been waiting for the marriage day? Ever since Adam fell. They have been waiting all these years for the manifestation of the sons of God. How long is it since Adam fell? I do not know exactly, but it is roughly some six thousand years. These heavenly luminaries have all this time been waiting for the day when Christ will come!

If they have been waiting patiently for six thousand years, it behoves you and me to be very patient. We are children of yesterday; we have only begun to be in this world. We must be patient until the coming of the Lord. We must establish our hearts in patience, waiting patiently for the coming of the Lord, because the return of the Lord will come to pass. Christ is even now waiting for the trumpet to sound; and when that happens, these words will be fulfilled.

In the meantime, says Paul, all eyes are upon you. The heavenly bodies are not interested in the unbelieving world. It is a lie to think that Christians are marginalized—it is the lie of the devil to discourage us. We are not to suppose that the unbeliever is the one who counts while the believer does not. Never believe it. The only ones whom the universe is interested in are the sons of God. The eyes of the universe are upon you who love Christ. They care for you more than they care for ten thousand worlds. You are the ones they concern themselves with. The earnest expectation of the creature is looking for your glory and your exaltation at last.

That is a very strong and striking picture, an amazing revelation! You will not get that on the television or radio.

You will not read that in the newspaper. Worldly men do not know these things because they do not read the word of God. But you and I know that this is true. We are encouraged to know it; God's word tells us so. It is the godly upon whom his eye is, and therefore the eyes of all creation also are watching out for that great day.

Let me give you an explanation for this remarkable fact. It is found in verse 20: 'For the creature was made subject to vanity, not willingly, but by reason of him who hath subjected the same in hope.' The universe in which we now live was subjected by God to vanity. When Adam and Eve were in paradise, in a state of innocence, all the universe was in perfect harmony; everything was perfect. It was a brand new universe. Nothing was going wrong. There was no curse; there was no hurt, no danger, no harm, anywhere. It was only when Adam disobeyed God by eating the forbidden fruit that God cursed the ground for man's sake. And that is the condition in which we are.

God put a 'vanity' into the material world. What does this mean? Instead of a fruitful earth, we have barren hillsides; we have the Sahara Desert. Dare I say that this would be true of a large part of the interior of the continent of Australia? It is the same with us in Scotland. The curse is to be seen everywhere. There are spots on the sun even! And so we could go on and on. Great holes are beginning to appear in the ozone layer. Ultraviolet light is coming in and causing cancer in man. We hear about pollution. Then there are volcanoes, tidal waves, floods, fires, forest fires. That is all part of the curse. The world is subject to vanity.

But, says the apostle, the created world was subjected to vanity 'not willingly, but by reason of him who hath subjected the same in hope'. There is a positive side to God's judgment on our sin. It is not a hopeless situation. It is not as though God has cursed the universe without any hope. Thank God, there is hope; and this hope is what Paul speaks about at verse 21: 'Because the creature itself also shall be delivered from the bondage of corruption into the glorious liberty of the children of God.' The universe round about us is going to partake of the coming glory. When, at the end of history, Christians are glorified with Christ, this universe also is going to be delivered from its bondage of corruption. It is going to escape from the present vanity and curse under which it labours. What will that mean? This universe is one day going to be beautified into 'new heavens and a new earth, wherein dwelleth righteousness' (1 Pet. 3:13). The curse will be over.

When Christ returns, the world will be rejuvenated or regenerated. It will be restored to its former perfection. More than that, it is going to be made the place of eternal happiness for all the people of God. Everything that God has made round about us will be liberated from the present condition of curse and vanity. This whole universe will again become a perfect environment for the people of God to live in.

What is meant by 'new heavens and a new earth'? That is a question which we cannot profess to answer with certainty. There is, of course, much mystery surrounding these wonderful subjects; but I will give you the best explanation that I know of.

The universe that we now live in is like a three-storeyed house. At the top is heaven; in the middle is earth; underneath is hell. But when Jesus comes back again in all his glory and we are united to him on the marriage day, earth and heaven will be joined together into one. Earth, as it now is, is the place of our probation. Here we are in a state of trial and test. But when Christ returns, the time of probation will be over. Everyone will either then be perfectly wicked in hell, or perfectly happy in heaven. There will be no place for the intermediate 'chamber' of earth.

It seems to me, then, that what God is telling us in Scripture is that heaven and earth will coalesce into one. It will be one new beautiful 'house'—one new perfect world; and it will be filled with beauty and glory. When you look into the new heavens and new earth there will not be a corner anywhere which will not speak of the glory of the Lord. Everywhere you look there will be signs of it. The Lord Jesus Christ describes the event as a 'regeneration': 'In the regeneration when the Son of man shall sit in the throne of his glory, ye also shall sit upon twelve thrones, judging the twelve tribes of Israel' (Matt. 19:28). The universe is to be regenerated, made new. The book of Revelation says,

'Behold, I make all things new.' 'And I saw a new heaven,' says John, 'and a new earth' (Rev. 21:5, 1). Similarly Paul in Romans 8:22 declares: 'We know that the whole creation groaneth and travaileth in pain together until now.'

There are different reasons why people may groan. The sick, dying and frail groan because of weakness. But a mother, about to give birth to a child, also groans, because of her labour pains. And the Greek word that Paul uses here conveys this latter sense. It is a reference to birth-pangs. The universe now is groaning, sighing and lamenting the evil condition in which it presently is, but these groans are not the groans of a dying universe about to pass away; they are the groans of a universe about to give birth to new heavens and a new earth. It speaks of a condition of hope.

The Christian is to be an optimist. He knows that this world is not going to be replaced by another. It will pass through fire in order to cleanse it, baptize it and purify it; but God will not destroy the present universe or throw it away. He is going to make it new. It will pass through purifying fires until all the filth is removed—and there is a lot of filth to be removed.

Soon the 'child' will be born—the new world. We believe in 'the new age'—not the New Age Movement that is popularly talked about, but God's new world. There is going to be a new universe. And the Christian is the only one who will be fit to enter it.

If you are not a Christian, I cannot pretend that your

condition is anything but terrible. You are in a tragic condition. You *must* come to Christ. He will have you; he loves to receive sinners. You are welcome to come to Christ.

You say, 'How do I come?' You must believe that he is God and the only Saviour of men. You must say to Christ in your heart, 'Lord, have mercy on me, a sinner.' If you do so, he will receive you, and he will bring you safe to glory.

This, then, is the destiny of the people of God. How different it is from the destiny of the wicked! All who are being sanctified in this life by faith in Christ will certainly and assuredly come to heaven at last. They will leave behind them all their cares and fears. Christ will give them a royal welcome. He will say, 'Come, ye blessed of my Father, inherit the kingdom prepared for you from the foundation of the world' (Matt. 25:34).

So all the people of God who are being sanctified in this life will come in that hour to see that he will glorify them with an eternal glory. They shall enter the palace of the King, and there they shall abide. Pray God that you and I may be there.

Other books by the same author published by the Trust

Great God of Wonders
ISBN: 978-0-85151-837-4, paperback, 240pp.

The Thought of God
ISBN: 978-0-85151-658-5, paperback, 256pp.

The Christian's High Calling
ISBN: 978-0-85151-792-6, paperback, 240pp.

Can We Know God?
ISBN: 978-0-85151-933-3, booklet, 32pp.

Finding Peace with God
ISBN: 978-1-84871-278-2, booklet, 40pp.

Some other books published by the Trust

Devoted to God: Blueprints for Sanctification
Sinclair B. Ferguson
ISBN: 978-1-84871-690-2, paperback, 296pp.

Help Heavenward: Guidance and Strength for the Christian's Life-Journey
Octavius Winslow
ISBN: 978-0-85151-775-9, paperback 212pp.

The Pilgrim's Progress
John Bunyan
ISBN: 9781848717466, small clothbound, 408pp.

Practical Religion: Being Plain Papers on the Duties, Experience, Dangers, and Privileges of Professing Christians
J. C. Ryle
ISBN: 978-1-84871-224-9, large clothbound, 480pp.

About the Publisher

The Banner of Truth Trust originated in 1957 in London. The founders believed that much of the best literature of historic Christianity had been allowed to fall into oblivion and that, under God, its recovery could well lead not only to a strengthening of the church, but to true revival.

Inter-denominational in vision, this publishing work is now international, and our lists include a number of contemporary authors as well as classics from the past. The translation of these books into many languages is encouraged.

A monthly magazine, *The Banner of Truth,* is also published. More information about this and all our publications can be found on our website or supplied by either of the offices below.

THE BANNER OF TRUTH TRUST

3 Murrayfield Road
Edinburgh, EH12 6EL
UK

PO Box 621, Carlisle
Pennsylvania 17013,
USA

banneroftruth.org